Getting Old

PUBLISHER'S NOTE

NOTICE OF RIGHTS

Contents

Mammographer
Susanne Braham

She twisted my shoulder,
contorted my torso,
and then she squished
my dinky boobs,
one teat at a time,
between two cold, hard slabs
and squeezed, and squeezed some more,
and yet some more,
until the vice was tightly set,
and then "Don't breathe!!" she said.

Holding seemed forever,
and being old as well as small
was just as bad as being young
or having lots to spare.

Six pix in all, but no recall
for which I was most grateful.

Back home that night,
extracted from a lock of hair,
I took this little sticky disc,
a marker that she'd firmly fixed
upon my shriveling nipple.

It's lucky that our cats and dogs
are spared this breast distress.
Imagine squishing three times eight,
every year, no less!

The simple act of writing this
feels much like tempting fate.

Ah, to have a beak! To grow feathers!

A mammographer is a modern, staunch
technician who deals with sweaty old
women barred from wearing deodorant.

take me to the aquarium and make out with me in the jelly fish room
Adrian Ernesto Cepeda

after a photo by Dmitrijs Belokons

Drop me from your soaked
and sweating pedestal as I push
your silver sterling cane aside
and put me up against this antiquated
glass, see through my deflowered
blouse that still breathes your beaten
name, gasping while I salivate
my favorite of those plastic wrapped
minty lips tasting for you; my already
netted my catch and hooked reclaimed.
No more fowl mood, I'm hungry
for your early bird afternoon special.
I want to feel your drying deviled tongue
explore my still wettest wrinkled sensations,
sprinkling of late December seasons tickling
me with your underwater shivers. Even
though your back's embraced I know you
can deliver. And maybe we'll rehash us
young by the waterfront Marlon Brando
and Eve Marie Saint like as you swam
dripping skinny towards the deepest

of my untouched regions, I remembered
you once treasured. Let us worship the spine
and tingling again and salvage those now
ancient across the pond love letters sent
par avion through enveloping red, white
and blue thoughts; let me salvage those
once longing vintage jackpots we somehow
dropped off at the Salvation Army. I long
to lick your distant eternal fountain pen,
again inked so divine as we uncover instant
waves, wishing your dog tagged nakedness
to reawaken me from your symphonic nap;
forget your fedora, surprise me arising
like a conductor and I will string along
your Hallelujah chorus memory.
Take me in this aquarium, splash us closer,
reaching clenched, we will be drenched
in smiles. Watch the jelly fishes eyeing
our pruning wrinkles, seems so simple
as shining skin imagines us as lovers
swimming through tanks clasping
our breath; reminding us, to not stay
in the shadows as ignored background
silhouettes. Let us drool so much louder
as our twice aching backs reawaken us—
and they will hear our once primal voices,
panting proudly, now becoming redefined.

When I Turn Eighty

Ann Howells

When I am old, I said, I will wear...
chartreuse, periwinkle, fuchsia,
be colorful as a box of gumdrops,
voluble as a goose. And, I am!
Fresh from my morning walk —
twice around the track equals one mile —
I check the pedometer strapped to my
  waistband.
Eighty, I tell you, *is the new fifty*,
and I natter on about the latest antics
of the man in 17E: *always something to gripe about*
that one, as I move with friends, en masse,
to the activity room.

Mahjong. Who'd have thought fifty years ago
I'd be playing this foreign game with women
who are almost sisters — close as sorority sisters
back in college, only, thank the Lord,
no communal showers. I've earned a little space.
I fondle tiles chamfered from passage
through calloused or lotion-soft fingers.
Rumor has it there's some hanky-panky going
  on
between me and the gentleman in 7N; I blush

when his name is mentioned but neither
  confirm nor deny.

I hear about Carol's new pacemaker, Janet's hip.
It's part of life;
whatever modern medicine has to dish out,
we nod, joke about bionic women.
Tell us how amazing we truly are.

Miss Frankie
Ann Howells

I see her pass the window,
stooped, shuffling in flickering lamplight,
pacing when restless legs allow no sleep.
The world quiets
as if all life is suspended,
and slippered feet wear dull paths
like sky maps
tracing a lonely planet's orbit.

A heart monitor strapped to her side
is baggage she must bear,
but she won't relinquish the cigarette
dangling from her lip.
She's buried two husbands,
five of eight boys.
She paces, pauses,
slaps card on card in endless solitaire.
Almost blind, almost deaf,
she pulls the TV nearer her chair,
turns it up again.
Too much trouble to wear her teeth.

But, one son brings mail, removes trash,
and one delivers groceries:

microwave entrees, bread, milk,
an occasional garden tomato,
and sugar wafers—*Lordy*, she says,
I do love them sugar wafers.
Damn doctors don't help none, she reports.
Talking on the phone plumb wears me out.
It's been a good life, but
if the Good Lord wants me, I'm ready.

Old Knees
Ann Howells

No ruby slippers, no pixie dust,
no magic carpet

to whisk me home. No rickshaw
or aged horse to plod

back to the barn should I drop the reins.
My knees spark and enflame;

dull creak of bone on bone,
squeaky hinge that cries for oil

or graphite powder.
Somewhere young girls

race wildflower meadows;
leggy blonds leap for Frisbees

scuffing sugar sands. Those days
are behind me... but

what wouldn't I give for one strong gust
to push me up the road and home.

Smack in the Eye
Ann Howells

Holding the needle at arm's length,
I jab again with spit-damp thread,
hand trembles, eyes cross.

The button hangs loose, shirt
not wearable, and time after time,
that freaking needle winks.

I wash my glasses, dry them
on my shirt-tail, return to the odious
aim and miss. TV blares:

starlet adopts an Ethiopian orphan,
singer shows a baby bump,
actor caught cheating on his wife.

My daughter snatches the thread,
pokes that needle smack in its eye.
First shot. She hands it back,

disappears. I attach a red button,
shrug, use same thread on blue slacks,
green socks, yellow pajamas.

Paret & Auty

Ann Howells

At twenty, she marries him. Elopes to New York. A sister, furious to find he has not been courting her, turns cold. Moves her bed to the dining room. Never speaks again.

Lovely bride, eleven years his junior — china blue eyes, wheat colored hair to her waist — installed in a fort on the Potomac. He buys her mahogany furniture — bureaus with marble tops, cabinets with leaded glass doors. He buys her a car of her own. This is 1908. She mends his clothes, makes jams and cakes to feed his sweet tooth, cries monthly as she rinses bloody rags.

He finds a widower — friend of a friend — who cannot care for a two-year-old daughter. He brings her the child. He builds her a home on an island — indoor plumbing, gas stove from Sears and Roebuck, gas refrigerator — while other residents use privies, wood stoves, chill butter in wells. Men mend nets; women bury their dead. He buys her a piano, an organ to fill the house with music. She mends his clothes, makes jams and cakes to feed his sweet tooth.

He dies at ninety-two. They have never spent a night apart.

The Ancient Flocks of Wilson Street
Bill Cushing

They flock
to the park
cloaked in black,
perched on benches in the Winter sun,
the bills of their ball caps, like beaks,
dip in and out.

Like grackles
surrounding bread crumbs,
the ancient Armenians
ease their emotional baggage —
too young to remember
but old enough to recall those
who lived through
or died from
the Turkish carnage.
Surrounding the tables
filled with scattered dominoes,
on Christmas eve,
the old men chatter
about the old country
and its new destruction,
moving and
connecting

the ivory bones
with brittle fingers.

This little plot is now
their patch of earth,
and as
territorial
as the chastising mocking birds,
they chase strangers
from the grounds,
children
from weathered monkey bars.

Ann and Rupert
Clifford Wieck

I
Ann calls me, calls me,
Across the years, her heart to mine,
After marriages, hospitals, poverty,
Affairs, a child that soured.
Oh, Ann, the one I struggled for,
made promises to. I needed you
to prove myself — my first poetry
A signature on a contract.
Where are you?
Why now?

Her voice is strong;
It wakes me.
I don't believe it.
Isn't it late in the day, Ann,
Isn't it so very late in the day
To ask me to keep my word?

II
Rupert's legs are leaking.
His kidneys have failed
and he refuses dialysis.
Fluid pours down his calves,

Rivulets down a cave wall,
soaking his socks and shoes.
"My feet are cold," he complains,
"My legs are swollen. Help me."
"Put your feet up, Rupert,"
the nurse tells him.
"It's part of your treatment
You need to keep your feet up
To reduce your swelling;
To stop your legs from weeping."

"No," says Rupert. "It's uncomfortable.
It hurts me, it hurts my legs.
I'm not used to it. I don't like it.
My feet are cold.
Help me. My feet are cold."

Cardioversion

Clifford Wieck

I
The speaker throws out a question:
"What were you reading at 16?
What book influenced you the most?"
I have to dredge up the angst of those years,
The mooning, the yelling,
The moaning, the melancholy
Of meaning of everything touching
The becoming of longing,
Sun on snow:
It is Salinger's *Nine Stories* read and re-read
Every day every week for six straight months,
My holy book all Junior Year.
He matched me, Buddy Glass, Jerome David,
Bleeding wound for bleeding wound,
Festering sore for festering sore —
I was Walt, the dead lover,
And the girl who loved Walt,
And the soldier who loved Esme',
And Boo Boo — oh, my heart, my passion —
Boo Boo! (I knew she was really
Boo Boo Glass).
I went searching for God
With de Daumier-Smith.

I sat in the bathtub when
The Laughing Man died.
I hung up the phone
When Arthur called back.
Catcher was my gateway drug.
Nine Stories was the horse,
The hero, the skag.

II
On her birthday I bought her
A crippled dog—
Mangy, scrofulous,
For which I paid good money—
And a blind cat,
Bringing closure at last
To my lover's son's suicide.

Arrival

Carol Smallwood

Aging arrived when
doors were held open
with that smile for the elderly.

When catalogs descended like
Alice's pack of cards:
large numbered
clocks, colorful canes
for independence.

Alford's Devotional and Guide to Poetry: The Psalms
Bruce Alford

1. The psalmist, in telling us, as he often does, what passed between God and his soul, lets us know what we may expect long before the death of our parents.

2. We come face to face with difference.

3. A woman asks for water. I will not close the door.

4. And she drops into a chair. Spider veins abuse her legs and I am walking here with the water. Now, I give her the glass. Glance at her clothes. Use has beaten them bare.

5. There are threads of meaning and potential that I can't quite understand.

6. My tear is a tune. My heart is a tabor.

7. And I have given her a drink for which she did not labor.

8. סֶלָה And she stares at it, illuminating here and there her face, that makes you think the tomb.

9. And she drinks the water and says *The Lord is good.*

   I have been young, and now am old; yet have I not seen the righteous forsaken, nor his seed begging bread?

10. I remember casting bread upon the water.

11. I feel old.

12. Come on סֶלָה you should have known not to live according to a song.

13. I followed rules for nothing, and I kept them in vain.

    Look on the glass, and tell your face...

14. Now, she drinks, and whitish rings around her

15. Irises shine.

16. Everyone, eventually, goes blind, yet

17. Wretchedness cannot go unnoticed.

18. She picks a quarter from my floor and believes that she has picked it off the ground.

19. She yells look what I found! (You could say that she is gone).

> *She is not here and where she is, I will call*
> *there. It becomes possible to change places.*
> —*Robert Duncan*

20. Call her the daughter of King Saul.

21. The madness between the two comes from the Lord my god look at her spotted, ropy hands; the eyelid entombed in its hood or those lines around her mouth, her marionette's jaw.

> *The glass will show you how your beauty*
> *wears...*

22. I have furrows of intellectuality, folds between the eyes and loosening jowls. I need some heavy help with my self-esteem and slow belief; I don't feel old but I have a human face. Permit me to imitate the drink that she longs for.

23. Carry me away.

She is not here and where she is I will call there
it becomes possible to change places.
— Robert Duncan, The Presence of the Dance /
The Resolution of the Music
from Shakespeare's Sonnets

"Look on the glass, and tell your face…"
— Look in thy glass and tell the face thou
viewest, Sonnet III

"The glass will show you… "
— Thy glass will show thee how thy beauties
wear, Sonnet LXXVII

Like Shit
Douglas K. Currier

An old guy walks into a bar.
He's older than both the bartender
and the waitress — together. He's
older than this downtown establishment
searching for an identity. He remembers
when it used to be a McDonald's
— always dirty, as if they couldn't find
anyone to clean. He's older than the bar
and many of the craft beers
they have on draft — this bartender,
this waitress.

They treat him like he's seven months
pregnant. They frown. They disapprove.
The old have no right to drink, no need
— they are almost dead. They treat him
as if a beer is a binge, a glass of wine
— a security intervention. They treat him
as if he wants to get sick and sleep
in their restroom. They treat him as if
he'd brought his duck, as if he can't afford
their eight dollar beer, as if he were
about to cry and forget his name.

Muse
Jennifer Lagier

With a hot flash and snarl,
the Menopause Muse
ascends from hormonal hell,
complains of chronic insomnia,
critiques my fresh scones
and vanilla bean coffee.

She triggers anxiety, writer's block,
weight gain, depression.
Leaves me cursing fallen bread,
broken egg yolks, cremated risotto.
Promises wisdom, motivation,
startling imagery and metaphor,
the seed of a block-buster novel,
then disappears whenever
I steal time to scribble.
Inspires tears, nostalgia for skin tone,
taut jaw line, animal energy,
insatiable sex drive.

Annoyed at my lethargy,
she suggests I straighten up,
make a gratitude list,
start a new poem,
go weed my garden.

Gritting my teeth,
I pray for patience, sanity,
sip black cohosh tea,
take a cold shower.

Camille at the Medicare Workshop

Jennifer Lagier

As the consultant
draws on his
flip chart,
blathers on
about drug plans,
deductibles,
Camille practices
five sets of kegels.
Craves margaritas
or martinis,
maybe a nooner.
Wishes her damp panties
were a reaction
to arousal
rather than laughter.
Observes saggy
old women,
pot-bellied men,
in the chair rows
around her.
Wonders why
65 juicy years
have ambushed
her patience,

tautness, libido.
Blows off
this workshop.
Sneaks out
the back door.
Fires up
a big doobie.

Camille Morphs to Crone

Jennifer Lagier

Watch her balloon
before your eyes.
Slender ribs disappear
under pasty flab.
Her sexy growl
sounds more like
deep smoker's rasp.
Goddess breasts deflate,
unused, untouched,
nipples no longer perky.
Juicy nights discontinued,
fairy tales from the past.
Bikini wax unneeded,
not worth the trouble.
Everything down there
in deep hibernation.
Time hasn't been kind.
She wakes late,
arthritic and cranky,
with leg stubble,
mattress hair,
more wrinkles,
overpowered
by her own
morning breath.

My New Libido
Art Heifetz

My new libido's
frisky as a pup.
I mix into his food
a little ginger
maca root and arginine
and he's up for anything.
The old one wanted to
sleep all day.
Even the smell of
fresh meat sizzling on the grill
couldn't get him excited.

Getting Newly Old:
Another Parallel Poem
Changming Yuan

you can only talk
about what you used to do
and do
what you used to talk about

you shrink in both ways
and both ways are
the only way
to shrink

what's supposed to be hard
softens like a boiled noodle
what's supposed to be tender
hardens like a winter stone

one attempt
on top of another

or, one attemptable night
after another

Converting to Vegetarianism
Changming Yuan

now eating nothing
but tomatoes, potatoes
carrots, cabbages,
apples, watermelons
cherries, strawberries
sorghum, pepper
i recognize them all like true communists
either in appearance
or in heart

while their lycopene may contribute
to the well-being of my ischemic heart
i can only draw bloody memories from them
about summer fields
about all my red pasts in China

Aging

Changming Yuan

The other night, we were still imagining
How to grow old together, wondering what
Else to do besides making love in bed

But now, both of us have become really old
Older than our parents when we were young
Younger than our children who are getting old

While you feel wind-dried inside out, I find
Myself softened at both ends. Indeed
In a cold night like this, isn't it nice

To have someone to stay close enough with
And keep each other warm on this bed?

For Want of Red
Ruth Sabath Rosenthal

I see men ogling red-clad women: see-through-
cheap red — backless and sleeveless, breast-
tight, cheek-taut. What ecstasy, peeling layer,

after layer of red, the glistening ruby-ripe cores
revealed. Oh! to see those bodies in red slink
past "All You Can Eat" to "The Pink Pussy Cat"

down the street, to nosedive into hardcore
fantasy, rock and roll in it! Hey, in the thick
of it all, the stud-wannabes appear master-

fully cool — slick cucumbers escaping
getting caught red-handed eye-balling
each eye-catcher. In the dogged pursuit

of red, the cocksure voyeurs invariably
return home, likely without the slightest
shred of red showing. My old man,

a looker from way back, comes home, more
often than not, looking quite in the pink.
Home to me, his postmenopausal wife

whose red-faded dress grows more
threadbare daily, eyes bloodshot, bawling
over the tear in our state of union.

Forbearance worn thin, I look to my spouse
to redress despair — at the very least,
notice me. The louse looks my way,

turns away.

Now Voyeur
Ruth Sabath Rosenthal

This old heart of mine no longer beats
down the doldrums, nor turns humdrum
bright as gold, as it did in my prime;

and nightly, in dreams high in my vessel
of wanting delight, it's strangers acting
out *my* desires! Imagine that! Intruders

beating me to the punch in the quest for
hot sex: Moist bodies embrace, legs, twixt
& twain, heighten each twist & turn

of a lusty mind. And this morning I wake
far from all right, vowing to lotion my loins
daily, perfume my skin and, if my old man

again says, *Not tonight*, I'll write this
craft of mine, shove it in his face, and ride
out the current into the sunset

with as much grace as I can muster.

The Shoes of the Old Man are some Clunky Slippers
John G. Rodwan, Jr.

Earlier, pre-retirement, let's say,
his shoes were leather and said
this is serious footwear
for serious business
in serious office buildings.

Or, on weekends, or rare off days,
his shoes were racing-striped
with reflective bits and rubber treads;
these said: *I can run for miles,*
for long distances
on early morning streets.

Now, with hair thin and grey,
he prefers shoes with padding,
plenty of support and thick,
cushiony rubber soles;
shoes that say: *I think I'd rather*
just sit for a while.

Muse Interrupted
Mark Antony Rossi

There's nothing worse
Than writing poetry
On my old iphone
While pooping
My life away.

Who can concentrate
As their bowels become a volcano
Actually vocalizing
Its disagreement
With your dinner selection.

Hell is Genealogy

Mark Antony Rossi

Her dark history made him shiver
there was nothing he can do
nothing he could give her
so he drank and dreamed
and drowned his liver
until they found him flat down
floating in Grey River.

When I Was Young

Sarah Brown Weitzman

When I was young
our radio was a substantial piece of furniture
and the telephones had a rotary dial.
The refrigerator freezer was the size of a
    shoebox.
My father wound his watch every evening
    before
he went to bed. His La Salle car had a running
    board.

At the movies there was a double feature, one
coming attraction, a newsreel and an aged
    matron
with a flashlight who shined it on you if you
    misbehaved
and hauled herself up the stairs when the boys
in the balcony threw their chewed gum down
    on us.

When my grandmother died a telegram was
    delivered
right to our front door by the brother
of the girl who worked in the 5 & 10 cent store.

Everyone wore black to her funeral even though
they weren't related. My mother said the word,
divorcée, in a whisper when a cousin arrived.
Copies of the death certificate
were made with carbon paper.

I remember when our doctor made house calls.
A dollar allowance went a very long way
because with a penny I could buy twenty jelly
    beans
or a long strip of candy dots on paper.
My mother believed that steak was good for me.
Nothing we ever bought was labeled "Made in
    China"
and poems rhymed.

Things Have Gotten That Bad
Sarah Brown Weitzman

I used to be able to conjugate
irregular French verbs.
I used to know what a diphthong was.
Now for all I know it might be the bottom
piece of a swimsuit.
Things have gotten that bad.

Was it really possible
that I once was good at algebra
and actually appreciated axioms in geometry
for their relation to reality?
Lately when I draw parallel lines
of make-up liner
they converge and drift
over puffy sacks around my eyes
like some non-Euclidian's concept
of a different universe.
Things have gotten that bad.

Enough about the brain.
Remember those National Geographic photos
of primitive tribes, the old women
as though aging reversed a woman's body.
Things have gotten that bad.

And it gets worse
because one could hide
a lot with clothes
but I'd have to wear a veil or a mask
as my nose has widened
my eyes are smaller
my ears are bigger
my skin thinner
my lips thinner
at least my hearing's good
Whad ya say?

Rhyming Rita and Silver Sam
Lynn Hofman

Rhyming Rita's watching Silver Sam
she likes to watch the old man's muscles,
vines, she says smaller harvest, sweeter fruit
she's couched just so, a pillow here
a cushion there. he walks slowly, naked,
smiling as if time were no thing at all.
(Sammy knows about time, seen his share
likes it every way but empty).
he kneels and draws the lines of venus lightly
with his fingers, skating figures on her warm
  skin.
she gathers him in, he fits just so you know
he kisses lips and neck and breasts and belly
he's an avalanche, our Silver Sam
down Rhyming Rita mountain.
at the base, at the very thinness of
her thicket he brushes the brush and whispers
away and talks in tongues his story starting
slow, tilted, sideways, soft, barely there
then only there where there there
"no, go, slow, slow, oh, go, go"
says rhyming rita as sam delays and plays
in all the ways he knows.
it's later, she's lost count, he never started.

Rhyming Rita starts to cry, 'oh my oh why
i hate this fate, so late, so late so wrong it took so
long to find you' and Sammy says 'it's not so
    late,
and slow beats fast,
we only saved the best for last.'

– for dd

Big O
Lynn Hofman

Orgasm's an unruly son-of-a-bitch.
Loud, screaming, pushing and kicking its way
Out of the belly and down the dick.
It's a Heavy Metal Battle of the Bands
The big Express Train blasting out of the Tunnel
Into Sigmund Station.
It's your best friend,
The one with the bad manners
Who always gets invited to dinner anyway
Because he tells the sweetest stories.

Until
sometime in your late forties,
or after the first divorce.
Then things change.
Then Big O's a long procession of lascivious
    monks
chanting gregorian and slowly making their
    way
to the top of a mountain inside a cathedral.
Or it's nine innings of well-built baseball
Or a whole bottle of Ornellaia that dances
with greedy hips and sculpted shoulders
All the way through dinner.

And all the hooting of it
That used to keep the birds away
Turns into the lipsmack chirp
That calls them in.
Then you come like the ocean instead of the
  storm.
Imagine that you decide to stop for a while.
Maybe
She's had her little death
And she wants you to come die inside her
And you say that
Maybe
You and Big O are going to
Take a nap now and save the rest
For later.

Hands and Feet
Lynn Hofman

I don't own a lot of mirrors,
So feet and hands are the body parts I know
    best.
Feet stick out of my pants, they point to the
    Phillies' game on television
And they make a pair of brackets for my dick
    when
I'm lying in bed naked and thinking about that
    woman I met last December at Monks Cafe.
Hands, they chop an onion, type this, wave
    goodbye, and so on.

About a year ago, I saw some spots on my
    hands.
Freckles I guess, brown like October's oak
    leaves.
I'm not much into critical self-examination
(a lack that may have doomed a marriage and
certainly foreclosed my career as a mystic),
which is sort of like repeating
that I don't have much in the way of mirrors
but when I saw the spots I took a step-back look

at my hands
to see what I would feel.
What I felt was nostalgia, a longing for home.
What I saw were my father's hands, striated
   finger nails, crepey skin, leopard spots.
Foot check?
Well, yeah, a few bumps, a memory of old men
   wearing rubber sandals in the steam room and
The word 'bunion,' which always sounded like
   something that needed cream sauce, came to
   mind.
My father again, a 9 ½ Eddy in Florsheims.

Yup. It's me, getting my Dad on.
I'm the age that he was when I was 23.
Between then and when he died four years later,
   we moved our hands and feet
Through a cyclone of rage, reconciliation, pity
   and even, finally, love.

Hey kid, let's sing:
something's afoot, give the old man a hand.

memory challenge
Lynn Hofman

remember those three years we
were in english class together
and you were dating somebody
and i was dating somebody else?
remember how we debated
romantics, enchantics, the one and donne?

remember those seventeen years we
spent together raising kids
spackling walls counting the coups
on refrigerator magnets taking
those little risks that opened the throat,
the heart, the self-secret membrane?

okay, we didn't. i made that up
we met last christmas,
we're web-site wonders.
a week is a year, today's a month
there's not so much at stake
we could afford to lose it all or
we could win the big one win
and we could fold the time back now
we 2 could make magic, remember?

Sleeping Bags
Sarah Henry

A sign on the wall
of the laundromat
reads, "Sleeping Bags-
Fifteen Dollars"

I'm glad I don't own
a sleeping bag anymore.
No need to toss and turn
on the lumpy ground
while bats and bears
circle in teams.

Where are all the young
campers' sleeping bags today?
They must be sodden, green
bunches spinning in public
laundries like this.

Now I read in my bed
of flannel sheets and new
blankets. The mattress is firm
but somewhat yielding.
It has been recommended
by an orthopedic surgeon
for my aging back.

Single-Poem Poet
Anne Harding Woodworth

*"… true is the love bestowed upon the choicest
songs of our 'single-poem poets.'"*
    — Charles F. Richardson (1851-1913)

I'm in my nineties and would'ya believe it? —
This is the only poem I ever wrote.
Done just about everything
a guy can do in all these years:
put cherry bombs in mailboxes
and spent a night in jail,
seen twenty-three countries,
learned ancient Greek, Italian, and German,
walked in rice paddies, flown solo,
married Rosey, had a little boy. Why, I even
watched the U.S. soccer boys beat England
in the '50 World Cup. I've skied Alta,
laid me down in front of the White House,
spent another night in jail,
buried my Rosey, had a bypass,
dated a cousin of Marilyn Monroe.
I've had thirteen jobs, been fired once,
been in a hurricane, and dug at Vindolanda,
where I unearthed a strigil
that's in the British Museum.

Still, I never wrote it down till now.
And you're my witness, stranger,
the others being gone
who could've vouched for my poem,
even sung it, set it to a tune.
Maybe you will love it — truly —
my "Star-Spangled Banner,"
my "Old Oaken Bucket."
I'm a single-poem poet,
getting my song in just under the wire.

The Woman Who Hands You A Gun
Judith Arcana

Don't think because I'm old
I'm not learning anymore. No.
That's not how it goes. Right
now I'm on my way, leaving
town to be a carny, a barker
at the tattooed lady's tent flap
or the woman who hands you a gun
at the shooting gallery or hoops
to toss over baby dolls. It's got
to be something I don't have
to study or practice, something
I can slip right into, on-the-job
training. Because I don't have
that kind of time anymore.
I'm saying I'll be an intern
an apprentice — not a student.
I don't have time for that.

The Spelling Test
Liz Dolan

Teach your brother to spell
Sister Caritas commanded.
So each night Michael and I
fifteen months apart, sparred
at the enamel table over
i before *e* and double *b' s.*

How I relished folding up
my sleeves like Sister,
tossing my braids
as if they were a veil
and stabbing his decieve,
occassion and bubles
with my red pen.
He'd rip the papers to shreds
and convert them to confetti.

Each session ended
in poisoned barbs,
You dumb ox, I'd hiss.
Ass kisser, he'd sneer.

Today through a trach,
my brother spits out muddled syllables

his left side paralyzed, his lips trembling.
When I massage his neck
and shoulders, I test him still,
Are my fingers here or there?
He's unable to feel the pressure.
I wipe the sauce dribbling from his chin.

Punctuation

Judith Arcana

With these creases down the sides of my face
everything I say — now — is a parenthetical
  remark.
Everything you see on my face is a parenthetical
  expression.

The softly cross-hatched lines under my eyes
tenderly echo those deep, permanent curves.
  They
set off all I'll ever want or hope or need to tell
  you in commas.

Looking at an Old Man
in the Pleasant St. Tea Room
Kevin Carey

He holds his hands against his chest.
I just got a haircut, he yells to no one
and no one answers. There are moments
when he smiles, almost chuckles at something
that flashes across his screen.
I know that will be me someday (if I'm lucky).

What will I remember?
—a game of spin the bottle,
catching frogs with my first dog,
a snow fort as big as a house,
a slow dance in high school,
my dad holding my hand at Fenway Park
and a man I can't see yelling *popcorn*.

My mother remembers things
she can't tell me,
she says did you hear the good news ?
and then grows quiet trying to think of what it
   was.
The other day she wrapped half a sandwich
in a napkin and asked me

to give it to the man on the television.
She doesn't know it's hard to see her this way.

Is it wrong to want someone to lie down
and go to sleep forever?
I make that wish
with the idea that she'll be with my father again,
the two of them on some tropical island
dancing after dinner, a jazz trio killing it softly.

We all wish for something — the other choice
that Socrates says is not the long dreamless
   sleep.
Maybe she is already there,
one foot in the water,
connecting to that place
where we can feed our TV heroes
when they are hungry,
that place where everything we remember
is just happening.

With Dad
Bill Cushing

Gone and now cremated,
I wait for my sister
to meet me at his now-
once bungalow. Searching
through the remains,
sifting among clothes
he left behind,

I put on a jacket
hanging in the closet,
turn toward the mirror
on an opposing wall.
I see gray hair and a beard,
half a century old,
but below that,

the jacket swallows
the child: its shoulders end
at my biceps; the cuffs
of each sleeve brush
against my knuckles.
Blushing, I remove the coat,
turn back to the closet, and

return it to its rightful place.

No Cure
Margaret Stawowy

> *If there's any illness for which people offer many*
> *remedies, you may be sure that particular illness is*
> *incurable. — Chekhov*

She tells me that in order to treat
my mother's Alzheimer's,
I must give her melatonin, Vitamin D,
serve green tea. She should meditate,
never eat carbohydrates, exercise four
days a week. Next, buy her a book
of crossword puzzles, drizzle
coconut oil on ten sides of veggies
to be eaten twelve hours apart but
at least three hours before bedtime
during which time she should study Chinese.

But my mother doesn't have Alzheimer's,
I tell her. Only age related cognitive decline —
just a little forgetful.
After all, she is 89.

Does she have diabetes?

No.

She sighs. "Old age is so unpredictable."

What I want to tell her:
Old age is very predictable —
that we will all die
(my mother, me, even her),
and for that,
there is no cure.

Grandma Wars
Carol Murphy

A war has gone on for decades, but no one ever talks about it. Quiet, spiteful skirmishes can go on in all families, even the outwardly Norman Rockwell types. A seething enmity will develop, but because open hostility can create family disunity, covert operations will suffice. Thus, deceptive but deadly glances and mazelike verbal exchanges that cannot be labeled as blatant battles will result. Senselessly some scuffles may even occasionally explode into actual legal conflicts. Mostly, however, the frays simmer like witch's brew. It's called the Grandma Wars.

I can still remember vividly when my Momo (mother's mother) leaned in close to my mother while my other grandmother, Nana, was talking to my father. "I always thought she was nuts," Momo whispered just loud enough that I heard it too. I was 10. My mother smiled and took a puff from her cigarette. Cigarettes were how she emphasized things.

Most parents' lives are too frantic to tune into these battles. And anyway, they can't afford to care that much. They just want help, even from feuding grandmas.

The war progresses in stages. Stage one is when the baby is born. The firstborn grandchild has the most potential for causing friction because he or she is first, a tiny little bundle of genes from both sides. And, of course, the first bit of friction is typically about who the baby looks like.

"Oh my god! She looks just like aunt Tillie!" says grandma one emphatically.

"No, she looks like my cousin Elva," says grandma two just as emphatically.

This happened when my first grandchild was born. Everyone on my side of the family claimed the baby looked just like people on our side. My husband would walk down the hallway where all our relatives' pictures hung, point out various folks and claim the baby looked like so many of them it made my head spin. Finally, he took me to one picture and said, "Look, she looks just like me!"

Well, she did, sort of, kinda, mostly.

But then, my daughter disgustedly told me that the other grandma said that the baby looked like a sister or an aunt or the father, never acknowledging the fact that the baby even had the same hair color as her very own mother.

Both sides were battling over a newborn's looks!

In an effort to call a truce, I collected all of the baby pictures on both sides and made a collage with the new grandchild in the middle. Actually she looked like all of them. But hey, don't all babies look alike?

The second battle comes with how to raise the child. This entails so many variables like sleeping routines, clothing, formula versus breast milk, diapering, when to introduce food and just about anything else that can come up.

When I was a baby, my Momo decided that I had to be dressed to the hilt. She could afford about anything she wanted to buy so, as my mother told me, whenever there was a family gathering, which could mean just about any gathering, Momo would buy special clothes and come over early to put me in them. Once my Nana had knitted me a sweater and when Momo was out of the room, she put it on me. When Momo came back, she took it off.

"Oh, mother!" my mother sighed, puffing madly on her cigarette. "It is just a sweater."

"It doesn't go with her outfit," Momo said to my mother. But to Nana she smiled pleasantly and said, "I thought it was a little hot in here."

Anyway, that's the way my mother told it, but I was told this went on and on.

I saw a YouTube video the other day that was actually shot in the maternity room of a hospital after the baby was born. The grandmothers were arguing about taking pictures of the new baby and wanted to keep changing his clothes to put on what each had bought him so they could take a picture of "their" grandchild. The baby was crying, the mother was crying and finally a nurse came in and asked the grandmothers to leave. Out in the hallway, one grandma punched the other one.

It's funny, but if you think about it, maybe not that funny.

This stuff starts really early.

In our family, hair has been an issue. How long it should be, when it should be cut and how it should be cut. My Nana had beautiful long thick hair she'd braid and wind around her head like a tiara. My Momo had thin stringy hair.

My son got my Nana's hair.

By 2, he had so much hair, he could have been in the stage production. Both sides of the family regularly made comments. Of course, he was the first great-grandchild.

Nana would say, "Let it grow."

Momo would say, "He doesn't even look like a boy."

My parents would roll their eyes and light cigarettes. They had gone through this with me. I too had my Nana's hair.

These battles are generational.

Who has the best grandma qualities can be the

next clash. In my family, who is the best cook is a battle. Now, I wouldn't really care because honestly I don't like to cook, but the other grandma fancies herself as a real gourmet chef and I have to say, this pokes me in a maddening way. I cannot compete with homemade bread, home grown then canned berry jam, or sautéed vegetables that came from her garden. I had a garden once and the ground squirrels destroyed it. Once is enough.

And she does it all so sweetly too. "Here," she says at every family food function, "try this." And she will point out some concoction she had made with her own two hands after she had planted, watered, grown, picked and cooked it "just for today."

Most times I will try whatever it is, and grudgingly I have to admit that she is a wonderful cook. However, to make matters worse, my husband raves over her baking. At the last holiday he even disloyally brought home some of her homemade pie. Ugh. Men and food!

So I fume and talk to my friends and find out the wars are going on everywhere. Many of these women even have scars left over from years of awful squabbling. I am relatively a newbie in these battles.

Some of my friends try to give me advice, but I see their conflict-weary bloodshot eyes and the grim downturn of their mouths. Maybe peace is unattainable.

But then the other day at my daughter's house I watched the other grandma kiss the baby and say "I love you" and I knew that baby needed both grandmas to say that. She needed both grandmas to give her hugs, play with her and love her in that special way only grandmas can do. Too much of the world is made up of broken families, maybe families where there isn't even one grandma.

And so that is the end of this war.

Well maybe…until she makes some perfect biscuit out of wheat she grew, cultivated stone ground then turned into lovely baked puffs.

My husband will want to take some home.

The Gift
Diana Decker

When given the life
you didn't ask for
you accepted with a weak smile
muttering thanks
not wanting to seem rude
wondering silently
what you would do with it
where in the world you would put it.

It was a gift, after all
so to make the best of the situation
you set it in a corner
keeping it on the off chance
that it had a value
you might have overlooked.

Years of tugs at your sleeve
drifted in the windows and settled on it
you wiped the dust with an impatient sense of
  duty
and very nearly missed the moment
that the sight of it caught you up short
in a begrudging, grateful smile.

What Now?
Adam D. Fisher

A man slowly walks the path
in the park, holding his
dog on a leash.
An hour later he sits on a bench
looking out at the pond, his dog
sniffing at his feet.

This is Monday — the first day he's retired.
He looks at the water, stands,
then sits and looks out again,
considers stocking up on cereal,
and oh, he could buy a few stamps
to have on hand.
He checks his watch, thinks
he'd be at his desk.
Wonders, what now?

Women of a Certain Age
Lu Pierro

Women of a certain age are an acquired taste.
Their plumage may be graying,
or they're thickening at the waist.

Beyond what can be measured,
are the pearls that lie below.
They'll love you with great pleasure,
with the gifts they can bestow.

Comfortable in negligee,
leather, or finest satin;
if you play their melody,
they'll sing for you in Latin.

One Shade of Grey
Keith Stewart

The fact I am aging has not escaped me. I can see it happening. I can feel it happening. Heck, I can even hear it happening.

Clearly, there a few lines at the side of my eyes when I smile or laugh. There are also some creases in my forehead when I look surprised or sneeze or do nothing at all. All of that can easily be wiped away by my little friend named Botox when I feel the wrinkles have crossed a line (no pun intended).

My hands are beginning to look like those of a middle-aged accountant's. What can only be described as two "age marks" have started forming there — splotchy, unsightly dots — while at the same time, the skin seems to have loosened up considerably. My feet, on the other hand, have hardened into two unbreakable paddles covered in leather so rough, it can cut you. But, these are issues a laser treatment or two can fix in a jiffy.

My body now aches to warn me of impending rainstorms or to inform me on things such as its refusal to function the next day if made to sleep on anything other than a Tempur-Pedic mattress. Sometimes it hurts for no apparent reason at all, just because it's cranky. All the small injuries that I compiled during my years playing tennis have led my body to betray me with fused bones, throbbing joints, and swollen tendons. Again, this is something I expected would happen, and, as any budding old fart would, I sort of like being able to say, "My ankle is killing me, that means it is going to storm tonight."

My knees, elbows, ankles, hips, and neck all crack and pop incessantly. Night and day. 24/7. If some part of me isn't popping or snapping with each step I have taken in the past year, I don't know about it. At this point, I have a regular routine I perform on myself to make sure all my joints and limbs, and any other movable part on my body, have popped before bed.

I have developed the very annoying habit of grunting, "OH!" each time I raise up from a sitting position. I realize all this snap, crackle, and popping probably has a lot to do with being overweight, and because being overweight is not the subject being discussed, I will gloss over it. (See how easy it is to ignore weight-related issues!)

As you can see, I have a pretty healthy grasp on the fact that I am now middle-aged. I gladly acknowledge all the above-mentioned conditions. I fully realize I can no longer eat a pizza at 1:00 a.m. without dire consequences. My idea of "going out" now involves being in bed asleep by midnight. But, nothing, and I mean nothing, could prepare for what I saw as I showered this morning.

A grey hair.

A grey hair DOWN THERE!!

WHAT THE HELL?! No one ever mentioned hair in that area greyed. EVER!

The hair on my head started prematurely greying when I was 16 years old, so I am no stranger to hair dye. My chest hair started greying about five years ago, and I have seen many men with grey chest hair, so that was no surprise. But this, this was a horse of a different color (pun intended that time).

At first, I thought it was an errant chest hair that had just fallen and drifted down in the area where the "love hair" lives. Then I realized I was wrong, and it was actually attached to my person, paralyzing me in the shower. I couldn't move, let alone breathe. I suddenly felt my life flash before me. How has this happened?!

This is apparently some deep, dark secret that the Aging Lords do not want people to know. I am sure if people realized their pubes were going to grey, there would be a lot more research and exploration for Ponce de Leon's Fountain of Youth. I, for one, would donate money on a regular basis to fund such a search if it meant never again seeing what I did in the shower this morning.

Seriously, WHY AREN'T WE FUNDING THIS?

I know there are hair dyes for men's hair, mustache, and beards. I now wonder if they make a dye for the hair in your special place? Perhaps this could be a new business venture for me.

My shower ended like a scene from a Lifetime movie—me hunched down in the tub, crying a bit while the warm water poured over me. I think I may have thrown up a little bit in my mouth. I then pulled myself together and stood up, grunting "OH!" as my knees popped, grabbed the grey bandit, held my breath, and yanked out the hair from my nether region. If the old wives' tale about pulling out one grey hair and seven growing back in its place is true, then I have a lot to think about this week.

One thing is certain, manscaping is in my immediate future.

End of the Cold War
Barry Antokoletz

Way back in 1991, the first aftershock of my
big Four-O was the collapse of the USSR and
European socialism. The second was the sudden
decline of my father. In fact, the two events were
linked. The personal loss of all those satellites
sent my communist-born dad from his hyper-
phobias (fascism and fertility), through
hypochondria (tear-gassing and flatulence), to a
fatal revulsion against mental retardation and
me. He always suspected that I'd been a revenge
plot by the defeated Axis against America
implanted in a sabotaged condom. I do bend
slightly Japanese, am a lower achiever than my
older siblings, and, due to the excesses of Stalin,
often expressed a distaste for Dad's politics. He
called me a "bourgeois sentimentalist," a phrase
so above my head (I was always bowing) that it
almost sounded cool. Why, he even considered
me a traitor to the working class and thought
me worthy of my own KGB file. He certainly
talked to me as little as possible, and when he
had to, it was always in the third person. So his

proper name for me was *He*. By the same token, he raised me not to refer to him as Dad, but by his terrible first name, Ivan.

To his credit, he refrained from physically abusing me. Violence against the peasantry violated his Marxism. Instead, I was boarded, clothed, and shelved practically like a member of our family.

Therefore, the threat and promise of his demise always hung over me like the Great Universal Mystery. When, where, and how would it happen? Indeed, my musings about death invariably derived from my father, a grave spirit entwined with my own mortality. As disparaging as he'd been of me from the beginning, I reluctantly (we were both reluctant) came to realize during his final days that I was his farting image, his own second edition, a facts-of-life reality that surely lay at the root of his resentment.

As Ivan got frailer, I flirted with the other side of life: conception, pregnancy, and my own paternity. It was a one-night stand with Dohery of Oklahoma for whom happiness was a farmstead. "Hiya, Karl, how are ya?" she would sing, high and fast like a music-hall cowgirl. It was attraction, then opportunity, then a quickie during which I ranneth over. Two weeks later, she waived any late withdrawal penalty I'd incurred with a warble: "I ain't pregnant, Karl. Congrats!"

"You sure had me hopping. That nausea of

yours—"

"Just the company, I reckon. Anyhow, nice knowing ya." She plugged me a western handshake and departed with a sturdy indifference.

However, the affair proved me fertile, and the seemingly impossible loomed up at me, laughed, and begged off on this postcard:

Hiya, Karl, from my vacation in Salt Lake City. Guess what! Doing fine after an abortion. Hope you don't mind. Adieu. —Dohery.

A conspiracy against my reproducing? A hapless joke? I didn't laugh. She was a definite airhead.

Days after I would not be a father, Ivan got his diagnosis. Terminal kidney failure. Not one of us Graysonovas believed it because you weren't supposed to die before seventy-five. Ivan was seventy-four. He ceased to walk, then sit. Yellow jaundice replaced his Yellow Peril, and my childhood nursery became a hospice.

I envisioned a future without Ivan when I might look back at the present. I'd regret how I hadn't kissed him enough, visited him enough, taken him out enough, nor engaged him enough in his endless politics. Today, while I still had the luxury, my conscience spoke: *Jump into it with him, indulge him in the long-dead, outdated, irrelevant, rehashed discussions from that bygone Age of isms, of which he's so much a part. There's still time, Brother, before he's really left you forever and taken the whole Cold War with him.*

Home attendants surrounded him day and night, and they gave nary a hint that he ever asked about me. When I could hack my way through them to get close enough, I asked him, "How's the revolution shaping up?"

He ignored me. "Where's Josef?" he muttered about my brother, seemingly to himself. "He was here with his little boy."

"Josef doesn't have a little boy," I replied. "Rosa, she has the little boy. Brother has a girl. Do you need to see him?"

"He's my son, isn't he? A son is all I've got."

"And a daughter and grandchildren." I left off with that. No use aggravating his condition. Hard enough distinguishing his regular personality from his dementia. I merely added, "I'm here."

"But that's all the time." He closed his eyes and escaped—into redder pastures perhaps.

Over the weeks, his skeletal knees curled to his chest, and his gaze increasingly shut me out—until his condition got so bad that I believed he'd finally mastered the art of acting.

"How's Ivan?" Aunt Mini inquired regularly by phone.

"Fine," I answered every time.

Weary of being placated, she responded, "What do you mean, fine?"

"His toes moved again today, and his eyes turned when I talked." I didn't say in which direction.

One day I assured him that I would marry and reproduce. His eyebrow arched and an ear stirred. "I've had some flings," I said in one more crack at his approval. "Maybe Miss Right will be a red, and I can give you an improved, more progressive version of myself."

Approval denied. The eyes rolled away and closed, demoting me from third person to nonentity. Too much for him, this cramming my whole future into his dwindling life span. I could only satisfy myself that for the present, his chest rose and fell, endowing him with enough time to see me married.

For decades, I'd rehearsed Ivan's death according to a Hollywood agenda — an in-denial, wish-fulfillment fantasy of him as the ideal father who was proud of his son. Fair warning in the form of growling and a death rattle would come days before, accompanied by incipient family hysteria. Visitors would flock sobbing onto our estate from the Old and New Worlds. To the strains of a band in the garden, there'd be a vigil featuring the immediate Graysonovas seated in the foreground shawled around tea and crumpets, awaiting word from the doc upstairs. Josef would be on hand with a basin of hot water, rags, and whiskey, consoling Mother and me with tenderness.

When the news broke, an Oscar-winning

shriek would arise from the women folk. Me—I would faint, arise, and faint again (Best actor). Mother, tears in her eyes, would gather us all to her bosom and drawl, "Karl, your pappy was a good man. He told me to tell you how much he loved you, how good you were to him, and that he chose *you* to carry on his torch" (Best actress).

Late one night, my real mother phoned in. "We're expecting sleet," she reported.

"Thanks. I have boots for every winter condition. Now, what is it?"

"Ivan is finished," she said with a delivery so matter-of-fact that I nearly missed it for the weather.

"*Finished* could depend on one's perception," I conjectured in a shaky voice to change her mind. "What do you understand by finished?" Semantics had nuances. I'd been to college.

"He died at six p.m."

"You're saying, then, he's dead?"

"Yes."

"Why?"

"Because it's true."

"But he was only seventy-four."

"Old enough for him. Anyway, what's new with you?"

"My father just died."

"I know. Josef and Rosa were here all

evening."

"So where was I?"

"Don't go by me."

"I mean it took you five hours to call?"

"Don't raise your voice. With something this close to home and heart, one overlooks outside parties. We haven't even told Ivan's loved ones yet. But I'm the most upset. The linoleum man came today and left scraps everywhere."

"*That* upset you."

"How would you like to wallow in oil and dirt? Don't answer that."

"But your husband of half a century —!"

"Sure. But right now, I only know that hospital bed of his made cleaning in corners difficult."

"Are you alone?"

"Who would you expect at this hour, my paramour? Do you think Josef and Rosa can revel around here all night like they used to? They're married. And Ivan — well, he'll never be the same. You know."

"Mother, you shouldn't be alone on a night like this. I'll come and stay with you. Or would you rather I picked you up to come here?"

"Now, at this hour, you're arranging something? I just want to get to bed. It's been a big day. This damned mess." She hung up, leaving me alone in my semi-orphaned state.

After eons of inhabiting my little niche, clinging terrified to our asylum from the assaults of capitalist life, and stubbornly resisting history and his personal fate, Ivan, His Overwhelming Presence, my tortured figure of adamant immortality—was no more. At last, Mother Nature had commuted his existence and granted him his flying papers. No wind outside blew up, nor did lightning flash. My remorse turned to rage. There'd been a lynching. The one-time revolutionary had gone too gentle into his good night.

Didn't his widow need me, her son, at all? I flew instantly to her, hoping she'd break down, sm-mother me with affection, make me hot cocoa, reminisce with me through the night. I entered by my spare key (Ivan's) and found her mopping around his vacated bed. The body was gone, out of her way and beyond my reach, sparing me a temptation to touch him that might not have been sincere.

"No good for you to be out at night," Mother sighed imposed upon, in her habit of believing herself.

At Woodlawn next day, we Graysonovas held as civil a funeral to oblige Ivan's atheism as possible in the unreal world. It was presided over by a very reformed rabbi, "not too reactionary," according to Ivan himself, and attended by whomever was left of him—we Graysonovas, our in-laws, Aunt Mini, a neighbor, and one drop-in from Ivan's builder's union. Conspicuously absent by their absences was the Soviet Politburo.

In my childhood, I'd imagined him as a monster in our plumbing who would one day pop from the toilet and grab my hiney. So I composed this eulogy —

Whether cradle to grave or crib to crypt,
Materially, dialectically, dust to dust,
'Twas the sea bowl whence he came,
And the sea bowl whither he must —

and quickly withdrew it lest some devotee mistakenly sprinkle potty water over the open coffin. Instead, we had the rabbi quote *The Communist Manifesto.*

When most grievers had exited, I studied my mummified original. For the first time, I saw our remarkable resemblance — like staring into my own dead face. Here lay the would-be working-class hero who had made a pact with adversity. And here before his shell stood his resulting two-legged disappointment.

Then I marked the fingers intertwined on his belly. Having never looked at them closely, I now noticed their rough, labored quality. His passing suddenly made me realize what he'd been about all these years. A heretofore unconscious sensibility welled up inside me, and I realized who I was and where I'd come from: I was a son of the proletariat. With Ivan's cold war over, my class-consciousness was about to begin. Tearfully I turned to some indistinct mourner opposite me, nodded to the fingers, and whispered,

"Those are the hands that fed me."

By Both Eyes
Amanda Lewan

"Do you know what it's like to live in the dust?" he asked, inching his finger along the windowsill. Diane walked over and wiped the mark. She listened to her father's complaints, responding with a patient voice she'd practiced as her father's illness turned for the worse. His memory faded more with each morning. Often, he forgot whole sentences. He would pause and look out the window, turning away from what he could not understand. Words seemed to pass through him, floating into the air like flecks of dust. He broke long periods of silence with loud complaints. Diane wondered if he shouted only to test her, to see if she was still there, still near him in his chair by the window watching the day fade.

It was the beginning of spring when Diane's father first moved in. He couldn't be alone any longer, and no other sibling was up to the task. Diane worked from home, and they imagined she was very lonely with her husband away. It only made sense that her brother and sister asked her to take their father in. They thought she would be able to put up with him best.

"It won't be that bad. I'll be by to check up on things and help when I can," her younger sister had said. She had seen her twice since the arrangement. Her brother was a little better, stopping by on Wednesday nights for dinner.

In the beginning, things weren't so bad. Her father slept often and kept to himself in the guest room. Diane would cook dinner and afterwards they'd sit around together watching baseball or whatever sport was on television. He enjoyed sitting outside in the evening where he could watch the night sweep in. They had bonfires after dinner, and her father would share stories as best as he could. This was the pain of a storyteller: he was always on the edge of some new discovery, and only satisfied when he could find a way to share it. It hurt him to hold a dull image in his mind, begging for remembrance at the tip of his tongue. Mostly, he remembered enough of the story to create an ending, but Diane would step in and help him. Fall brought a silence that slipped into the house, but never a peaceful silence.

Today it was the dust. Yesterday it was the neighbor's cat.

"That cat. That cat."

"What is it?" Diane asked from the other room.

"That damn cat. CAT," he shouted. At the second, much louder shout, Diane hurried over.

She found the neighbor's orange cat wandering through her bushes.

"It's all right Dad." She placed her hand on his shoulder.

"It's not all right. It doesn't belong in our bushes."

Diane distracted him by commenting on the score of the game. Her father never left the house now, and she missed sitting outside with him on those first warm summer nights. She missed their conversations. All he wanted to do now was stay in the house, where he was safe with what might remain.

§

A red alert caught her eye at the bottom of the television screen. It was a special announcement, a story on an attack in Afghanistan. Diane felt her throat tighten and a weight drop down her stomach. A sick feeling grew inside her. Every day she searched the news, grasping for a bit of information, anything she could piece together to learn about that place. She had to force herself to stop wandering through the channels, remind herself that these stories were never completely real. What did they know about the soldiers there? No one knew except the men and women who lived there, who fought there.

She feared for stories like this one. It meant a rise in tension, an increase in fear, where the smallest trigger might release another attack.

More information was to come as the story wound down into the night's headlines.

She kept the news on, just in case, and finished setting the table for dinner.

"I made hot soup to help with your cold," she said, directing her father to the kitchen. "There are no peas in it this time, Dad."

"Well, thank you," he said. "I never liked soup much."

"I hope we hear something from him soon."

"What?"

"There's been bad news, Dad," she said. "Near Garret."

He was almost finished eating.

"Maybe the news will be on again tonight," he replied.

Diane wondered if he remembered Garret. She had reminded him several times in the past few weeks. They looked at her wedding photos just the other day. Her father smiled and told her how beautiful a bride she had been, but said nothing about Garret.

Diane cleared the kitchen and then helped her father change into his clothes for the night. She made sure he went to bed before she retired. Then, she sat up in bed, and pulled out her laptop to reread Garret's past email. All she knew were these words on her screen. She didn't know when she would get to hear from him next, if she would get to hear from him again. She couldn't stand not knowing. She wondered if he remembered the way it felt when he lay next to her, his warm press against her body, as they held each other in bed. She tried to think of the firm press of his body against hers as he hugged her goodnight.

§

Email Received

September 22nd, 8:07 a.m.

Diane,

I'm sorry I haven't been able to get in touch with you for so long. I probably can't call again for a while. You should know I'm doing just fine. We're getting more missions every day, and it's getting difficult for us to keep up.

You asked what it's like, but it's a world all on its own. Everything is brown, the same shade of brown. The earth, the buildings, the clothing the people wear, it's all covered in this brown. Most of the villages we pass through are half empty. People have already left the violent areas that we are now just entering, but there are always those left behind. They're the ones we have to keep an eye out for. Mostly, it's abandoned children.

The only beautiful thing is the poppy plant. It's bright and stands out in the dust. I've seen bright colors only one other time, when we were passing near a graveyard. They hang their clothing up in the cemetery. They tie it to trees or rope and hang it over the graves. From a distance it almost looks like the bright colored flags you'd see marking a sale. It always stands out wherever you see it.

From what I've seen so far, there are children everywhere. Yesterday I was walking with one of the little boys from the village, trying to understand his English. He wanted my pen. Many of them don't know how to read and write. They're fascinated with our pens because they stand for knowing. I'm glad to hear things are going well. I miss you and can't wait to be home again.

All my love, Garret.

§

Diane woke in the middle of the night to a loud noise coming from the kitchen. She felt her heart drop.

"Dad, is that you?"

The kitchen chair was knocked over, and her father had fallen. He was propping himself up from the ground in an attempt to stand up. His blue eyes were hazy as he stood there looking at her.

"Are you okay?"

He looked around and saw the kitchen chair on the floor. When he moved to bend over, he stopped. Diane was in the room with him and this realization surprised him.

"Help me up," he said to his daughter. "I was just getting water."

She helped her father up, slowly, and filled a glass of water for him.

"Are you sure you're fine?"

"All is fine."

He smiled at her, taking her hand as she guided him gently back towards the hallway.

§

It had been two days since the news of the attack, and two days without a word from Garret. This was not unusual; often a week would pass without any word from him. She tried to calm herself with the comfort that it was Wednesday. On Wednesday, her brother came for dinner. Tommy always brought over the ingredients. Diane cooked just the way their mother had when she was alive: snap peas, red onion, broccoli, and no carrots for Tommy. Everything always tasted better when her mother had made it.

Tommy came in and set the groceries down. He leaned in to kiss her on the cheek, and his father too.

"How are you doing, Dad?"

Dad nodded, not looking up at his son.

"And how are you?" Tommy asked.

"All right. Hanging in there," Diane

answered.

"I'm sure we'll hear from him any moment now," Tommy leaned in closer to her. "Has he been eating?"

"Yes."

Diane made hot tea for Tommy and offered some to their father, who declined. He was busy focusing on Tommy, listening as he spoke about his day and the kids. Tommy pulled out pictures from an envelope he had brought. Their school photos had just come in. He set them down on the table in front of their father, watching for a sign of recognition. Diane avoided doing that too often. Her father was losing the ability to tell their family members apart; at times he was frustrated with questioning, but other times he just smiled and let the images pass over him unable to discern the faces. This upset Diane and Tommy more than it upset their father.

"Thank you," he said to the photo, and placed it inside his pocket.

They ate dinner, and when they finished Diane cleaned up and walked Tommy to the front door. He always left right after dinner, but today she held him back a moment longer.

"Is everything all right?" he asked.

"I woke up last night and Dad was in the kitchen," she said. "He fell but he said he was fine this morning."

"He's probably fine," he said. "But just keep an eye out."

"What if it happens again? What if it's worse?"

"Just keep watching out," he said, turning to kiss her goodbye. "You're taking great care of him."

How could Diane keep an eye out for her father in the middle of the night? She felt unsatisfied with her brother's response, and worried more about their father's health each day. Her father was sitting by the window, looking out at the front yard. His hand moved slowly to wave goodbye at his son, but Tommy hadn't noticed. Tommy's truck was already driving down the road.

§

Email Received

October 5th, 3:16 a.m.

Diane,

I don't have much time to write to you today. We're all doing fine. No one has been injured, and I'm very happy how well we all work together. We're getting used to things. Some of the locals are friendlier to us, but most remain neutral to both sides. Yesterday, we removed an explosive that was in a vine near a house. The owner came out and looked around. He didn't wave or look at us at all, but walked right past us. It was strange to be unacknowledged.

I wanted to tell you that I've been learning a bit of the language, just a few phrases. They have some wonderful terms to show their respect towards one another. They use this phrase "By Both Eyes." It means to be at one's service, as if they are watching over carefully, in service of one another. It reminded me of you. You are an angel to your father. I'll speak the language to you when I get back. It's not very romantic, just to warn you. I miss you, and hope you and dad are doing well.

All my love, Garret.

§

There were times when her father's memory stabilized. She would hear full sentences almost linking to a story, but most of the conversation was on her end. She imagined her father listened, that his nods were reassurances of the truth, and that he was still there for her, helping her wait patiently for the return of her husband. They were both waiting together, watching the sunset from the living room window, when the phone rang. It was nurse calling with news that Garret was injured and resting.

Her father smiled at the news, a mouth wide with joy. "He'll be fine."

"The shot was in his left leg. It's infected pretty bad, and they need to monitor it closely."

Her father was still smiling.

"We just need to wait and see," she said. "Hopefully, we'll hear more soon."

"He'll be fine," he said again and then turned out towards the window, as if the case had been solved and the wound long healed.

At night they prayed for his infection to pass. At least, Diane believed her father never lost the words for prayer, and she reminded him to pray for Garret. He mumbled the word God once in a while, a thank you sliding out from his speech. She watched him close his eyes, moving his lips, and he made the sign of the cross, moving his wrinkled hands over a long, tired face. He prayed and then removed his thick glasses off of his face. He was nearly bald, but what was left of his hair looked like puffs of white clouds perched around his neck His prayers had always been acts of gratitude, a thank you in the midst of daily life.

§

Email Received

October 14th, 10:16 p.m.

Diane,

I'm so happy we got to talk. The sound of your voice reminds me of home. Tell me more about work. How are you doing? How is your father this week? How is your sister? Tommy and the kids? You don't mention them as much. I want to hear all I can about back home.

I know it's hard with your father, but you should see your friends this week. Get out of the house. Do it for me, while I'm out here and missing it all. Tell me what you're doing and everything that's on your mind. Things are getting rough out here. It feels tenser every day. You have nothing to worry about though. We all work so well together. I want to tell you so much more, but I can't talk about it right now. Please keep an eye out for me in the next week. I'll be able to get a day of rest again and am hoping to hear your voice.

All my love, Garret

§

Diane read his last email over and over. It was the last time he wrote to her before the attack. She had been reading his old emails the entire week since she first heard news of the attack. She read bits and pieces out loud to her father and she read to herself in bed. She did not let herself cry much, for she sensed her father's own worry and confusion increasing with hers. Diane wondered if he understood what it meant to not hear from Garret or the nurse for several days now. Diane was still waiting.

"He's a strong man. He'll take care of himself," he said to her from the chair, in the middle of a game.

She took comfort thinking her father remembered. When she felt better, she was up cooking and caring for her father with more consideration than usual. It kept her busy, and made her feel like she had something important to do besides waiting.

§

Another day passed and through her sleepless haze, she jumped at the sound of the telephone in the middle of the night.

"Hello."

"Garret. Are you all right? What's going on?"

"They're sending me home," he said calmly. "I'm going to be fine."

"I'm so glad," Diane cried. "I'm so glad."

"My tendon is going to need work. I need to come home for therapy," he paused. "I'm lucky that's all now."

"I can't believe you're coming home."

"Yes, I'm coming home," he said.

§

It was a warm day, unusually warm for the edge of winter, when Diane and her father greeted Garret at the airport. They had left early, Diane unable to hold her excitement. Her father had not said much in the car ride there, though his silence was so common she often forgot she was driving someone else too. Diane explained again what had happened to Garret. Her father only said one sentence during the ride: Garret is fine. The airport wasn't crowded and they waited as close to the exit as they could. Diane saw a man in a wheelchair exiting the ramp, and slowly recognized Garret. She had never seen him in a wheelchair and the sight startled her.

She leaned down to kiss him, putting her arm around him as he stretched his body forward from the chair. When she pulled away, she realized her father was staring at them.

"Dad, this is Garret."

"He made it home just like I told you," he said. "Knew you'd be fine, son."

In the car, Garret spoke with her father about the baseball game they'd be watching later. He reminded him who his favorite team was, and that her father never liked his team. When they came home, she helped Garret settle in with her father by the television, and she waited to make sure they were both all right. She left them in the living room while she prepared their dinner.

"No, not this team," her father shouted. "NO."

Diane felt the urge to run back to the living room, but paused when she remembered he wasn't alone. She looked out to check on him from a distance.

Garret reached over and put his hand on her father's arm.

"It's all right Dad, there's still a couple more innings to go."

Diane turned around, but not before she looked at her father to see his face smiling at the sound of Garret's voice.

She thought he must remember. He must remember and love him, too.

The Best Medicine
Sandy McPheron

The phone call I had expected for some time, finally came. "Mom needs surgery," my middle sister announced.

I wasn't surprised. My mother had been having the usual problems of an eighty-three-year old woman, but they had become more troublesome of late. My mother had, of course, let things go to the critical point rather than go to a doctor.

"When is surgery planned?" I asked, eyeing my calendar and mentally juggling commitments.

"The twenty-third of this month," replied my sister Grace, who lived with Mom.

"Okay. I can fly in two days before, and stay a couple of weeks if needed."

My body began to itch and break out in hives in anticipation of spending that much time in close proximity to my family. They know, and I know, that living 2,000 miles away keeps us all happier.

My husband and I have offered for years to have my mother live with us. We even, for a while, looked at homes with "Grandparent Apartments."

But, Mother has always broadly hinted that she knows my husband and I have different "cleanliness standards."

This is true. They are not hoarders, nor are mice sitting in the living room having cigars, but one summer when I was back for my annual visit I decided to run the vacuum around my mom's living room. It clearly wasn't picking up, so I took off the long metal tube to check for the problem, and sure enough when I poked a coat hanger through to the obvious blockage a large clump of pine needles plopped out… this was July. Either my family had taken to vacuuming the local forest preserve or had given up cleaning at Christmas because the vacuum got clogged.

On my visits I tried to ignore the dust bunnies under my bed that were the size of German Shepherds, but it was hard not to grab a broom or mop without looking terribly rude.

Also, I freely admit my general home maintenance standards are harsh compared to theirs. I like to get those broken things in life taken care of in a timely fashion.

When my mother's roof was leaking and the plaster in the powder room was crashing to the floor, if you wanted to use it she would call out, "Oh, honey use the upstairs bathroom, that one's not clean." Meaning I haven't gotten around to calling a roofer and there is ten pounds of plaster on the toilet seat, and you might get a concussion.

When her basement walls leaked, she chose to sop up the water with old bedspreads. She dragged them sopping wet to the utility sink with her eighty-five-pound body, and would ring them out for two years before calling the company to reseal the walls.

Finally, I found out she was using Chiclets gum to act as a tooth replacement for missing tooth, because she was afraid to go to the dentist. Now this is a woman that worked for a dentist while going to college, lives in a very nice northern suburb of Chicago, has good insurance, and is fully educated on the fact that dentistry has a new invention called Novocain. Thankfully my sister lured her to a dentist that my mother ultimately liked, but the gum company probably saw a significant dip in their sale of Super Saver Packs of Chiclets.

§

My husband claims the reason I'm so different from my family is that I must have bumped up against my parent's front porch in a reed boat during a flood.

As my plane descended into Chicago I felt myself slipping into my role as eldest sister, eight years older than my middle sister and ten years older than my baby sister. I had led the charge into adulthood. My middle sister had always idolized me as so cool and sophisticated with my Cher-like hair, miniskirts, and cool friends during my teen years in the 60s. The youngest had always felt I was bossy, but let's look at my life situation as oldest sister; I was expected to herd them along. "Mom says get in the car." "Mom says wash your hands for dinner." So who gets accused of being bossy? Me, and Mom comes out smelling like a rose during baby sister's therapy sessions. Baby sister even seated her therapist next to me at her wedding as if to say *Watch my big sister, she'll probably tell people where to sit. I told you she was bossy.*

Nonetheless, our family reunion was joyous, with the usual hugging and kissing, but with discrete scrutiny, as only sisters can. *Does she look older than last time? Has she gained or lost more weight than me? Is she coloring her hair to cover her gray?*

As my sisters and I were exchanging news of my travels, my tiny mother entered the room wearing a pair of loose fitting jeans, her beloved white turtle neck, and denim shirt. She was clutching her crotch like a three-year-old waiting in line to use the toilet at Target.

"Mom, why are you holding your crotch?" I inquired.

"Well it feels sort of like my insides are falling out and this makes it feel better when I'm up and about."

Glancing at my sisters, who were standing behind her, I saw them silently laughing and shrugging. I was very dramatically brought up to speed on Mom's medical issue in classic Mom style.

Yep, it's time to see the doctor when you feel like your lady parts are dragging on the floor. It makes it hard to push the grocery cart, hold up your uterus and check if the melons are ripe in the produce department.

Mom had a pre-op appointment with the surgeon the next day. My sisters and I attended to ask any final questions. I felt, from some of my research, that this surgery had some risks down the road, but it was clear they had decided on this as the best surgery, and they seemed content as Mom signed the necessary forms.

It seemed I was primarily there to hold the coats and purses, although I did pipe up and ask the surgeon how long he had been doing this surgery. I got a cold stare. *Oh so you are the bossy one*, I imagined him thinking. He replied curtly in a list covering his magnificent career.

For the next two days before the surgery, Mother and I talked and laughed as we drank tea and sorted through old photos.

I glanced around, planning a little house cleaning while Mother was upstairs recovering, and my sister was at work. There is a fine art to this kind of covert cleaning of someone else's house; it can't be noticed by the everyday occupants: Vacuuming, wiping out kitchen drawers, dusting tops of shelves and fan blades. Cleaning the dining room breakfront glass might be taking things a step too far as the glass looked almost frosted, and they might notice if it turned clear.

On the day of surgery Mom was rich with too many loving daughters buzzing around her, checking her into the hospital, constantly reminding the hospital staff to speak up because she was a little deaf, and that she was going blind.

We were shown to Mom's pre-op room, the hospital staff asking many questions. I let my sisters assist Mom in answering. Vitals were taken, they handed my mother a gown and surgery cap, and they left us. I realized my mother was going to strip down in front of me. I frantically looked around the tiny, beige, windowless room for something, anything to look at, but there was nothing, not even a damn TV. Could I gracefully withdraw, claiming a need for Starbucks? Should I start balancing my checkbook? I did not want to see my mother naked. I had never seen my mother naked.

One of my sisters was already helping mom. I was called on to guide her arm out of her camisole. I could see her holding the sheet up to cover herself, but it was just making things more difficult as we tried to put the gown on.

Finally, with a small sigh, she dropped the sheet from her tiny breasts and we slipped the gown on. I acted as if it didn't matter to see my mother naked, but it did. I did not want to know what I would look like naked at eighty-three. Although, judging from my current weight I'll lean more towards my fluffy Great Grandma Sugar than my tiny bird-like mother. My sixty-three year old breasts ain't great looking now, and twenty more years of wear and tear will really take a toll.

Several tense hours in the waiting room later, the surgeon met with us and assured us the surgery had gone very well. I just knew he was mentally sticking his tongue out at me.

The next morning the nurses gave us a rapid-fire, three-minute-tutorial on how to take care of our mother's catheter bag as they were discharging her that day. "If she feels the urge to pee there is a problem."

They popped my tiny mother in a wheelchair, jammed a stack of patient care papers in our hands, and waved goodbye while singing out, "Call if there is a problem." A burly young man jetted my poor mom down the hall toward the hospital exit while managing to hit every bump and crack in the floor.

Somehow we managed to get our little mother into my sister's SUV. Then we discovered that every street on the North Shore of Chicago is riddled with potholes we had never noticed before. We hit every one, with my sister calling out, "Sorry Mom."

We got her home, poured a little soup down her, tucked her into bed and drugged her with a painkiller. Since she never took anything stronger than a vitamin C, we figured she would be out for a while

We had gotten a baby monitor so we could hear her if she needed anything. Unfortunately, I found out my mother moans in the middle of the night as if she is trying out as a ghost for a large Irish Castle. This caused me to sit bolt up-right out of a deep sleep and sent me running to her bedside, only to find her sleeping like an innocent.

I became obsessed with her catheter bag, carefully watching the flow and measuring the output. I would even creep into her bedroom at night, with a flashlight, in a semi GI Joe crawl, to make sure urine was still flowing. I took her temperature each evening, monitoring her for any sign of infection.

Things seemed to be settling in nicely, when several evenings after coming home Mom called me urgently into her room. "I have the urge to pee," she said, concern in her opaque eyes. She knew what the nurses had said. I tried to sound nonchalant, "Oh I'm sure it's nothing. Let me get Grace, and we'll check it out."

I strolled out of the room. When out of her sight, I tore down the stairs to my sister's room calling in a loud stage whisper, "Grace, Mom has the urge to pee!"

Grace came barreling out of her room, "What? Hell's bells."

It was fairly late in the evening. Mom would not go easy to an emergency room out of sheer stubbornness, but we weren't sure how to fix things.

We walked into Mom's room smiling. "So let's take a look," said my sister, trying to sound casual.

We both got on our knees to take a good look at the catheter bag.

"It looks like there might be a couple of tiny blood clots in with the urine, maybe another one is stuck in the tube," I said.

Grace looked up at Mom from her kneeling position, "Okay Mom. I need to check your tube so I may need to look up at—" There was a long pause as my sister grasped for the right word. "—your who-ha!"

"I don't care, I just need to pee," declared my mother as she began to squirm.

We all began to giggle a bit.

I had gotten a small tub so we could disconnect the tube from the bag to check if urine was still flowing.

My sister carefully pulled the tube from the bag and there was no urine flowing through the tube. "Hold this while I look at the rest of the tube," she said, handing me the tube.

Our heads came together as we peered closely at the length of the tube. There did seem to be a couple of red spots in it.

"Try squeezing them, maybe they'll flatten and move out," I suggested.

Grace gave one a squeeze and a geyser erupted, golden urine spraying everywhere from the detached tube, like the fountains at The Bellagio Hotel. I had forgotten to hold the tube down into the tub.

"Thar she blows," I said. We all burst out laughing.

"Ahhhh," my mother sighed with contentment. Her whole body relaxed.

Later as we were mopping up the urine with large soapy sponges, Grace commented, "Well this was one hell of a bonding moment."

"Actually, Mom, it seems fair that after all the times you cleaned up after us, we clean up after you. I'm noticing something interesting as I clean this wooden floor, your urine seems to impart a beautiful golden hue. Do you think we should start a business bottling it, and calling it Granny's Gold, or would that be elder abuse?"

We all laughed until the job was done. Mom drifted into a deep sleep, too tired to laugh anymore.

This was what I wanted for her final years, my final years, and the final years of all my loved ones—laughter.

Of Sound Mind
Siena Milia

The decision was easy. It was going through
with it that proved impossible. Later they would
argue whether or not I was of sound mind when
I attempted to end my life, but that greatly
depends on your definition of sound, doesn't it?
What is it really? Is it a person that thinks
methodically, rationally about life, that makes
daily, mundane, decisions and pats themselves
on the back for having a good day? It's funny
that no one considered asking me if I thought I
was of sound mind at the time of my "accident."
I guess that may solve the argument right there.
But none of them understand, people like that,
in white, starched nurses caps and neutral
colored New Balance sneakers. They can't see
the danger that's all around them. They live soft,
padded lives of egg salad sandwiches and ten-
minute tristes in the locker room. They never
think you're listening either, when they talk
about what's going on outside this place. They
leave the televisions on, but none of these other
vegetables pay it any attention. The world out
there's gone to lunatics and insanity and we're
being wheeled around on warped linoleum

floors, and watched by small black-eyed cameras in the ceiling corners. I counted once, sixteen on my floor alone. There are eight floors, not including the lobby. You do the math. Like I said, the decision was easy. No sane person could live like that for long.

I spent weeks hoarding pills, swiping those little plastic cups from other unfortunate inhabitants. They are all too far gone to think of escape. They no longer look out the windows or skirt along the walls or lash out when the white-shirted strong-arms come in to stick us with needles. No. I was alone and this was the only way out. It was so simple, and yet so hard. You see, that's their job, their whole purpose, to keep us alive. And they are very good at it, so good that when I finally threw back all eleven mismatched pills they had my stomach pumped within the half-hour and I was good as new, excepting the wide Velcro restraints that kept me in my bed.

Two weeks later they made two fatal mistakes. Fatal for me, not for them. I pitied them. They would go one living their fat, squishy lives, so sure that they served a purpose, that they were doing any of us any good by keeping us so painfully alive. Mistake number one was assuming that my stint of good behavior on bedrest meant they could again let me roam the halls on my own. The second wasn't entirely their fault, but maybe we can call it divine intervention. Mid-way into July the central air conditioning went out with a bang and a fire in the south wing. For those next few days nearly every window on the floor was wide open and the staff slugged around, fanning themselves with crisp New Haven Care Facility pamphlets. If you ask me, this is the only use for those stupid things. They're full of tasteful lies and doctored, well-angled photos.

At eight o'clock that night I stood in the sill of the cafeteria window fending off a barrage of white-suited baby-faced men with a red-checkered napkin and a dinner knife. Some vague memory of bulls and a crowded stadium came to mind. I had quite the audience. All the other slack-faced inmates watched with their food dribbling from their lips. A few of them cheered, one fainted flat in a slop of Jell-O. Some were horrified, some confused, but most didn't seem to care. But me, I was finally free. I gave them all a wave and a bow for theatrics and let gravity do the rest.

I should have known it was a Tuesday. I should have remembered that the cafeteria overlooked the alley where the dumpsters heaped with sacks of soft, soiled Depends and three-day-old mashed potatoes. The garbage left on Wednesday, bingo day. I'd always hated bingo.

Heritable Traits
Carol D. Marsh

Some life-changing events, like a marriage proposal, come with fanfare. Some tiptoe behind you, waiting for a moment or comment or glance to sidle into your consciousness. Take, for example, the way I found out I was going bald.

On a January 2014 evening, I happened to glance up at the security monitor over a take-out restaurant counter, its screen divided into four squares, each giving the view from a different camera. One of the cameras was situated behind me and I realized that was me on the monitor screen. I shifted a bit on my feet to make sure. Monitor Carol imitated me. I scratched my arm and monitor Carol had an itch in the same place. This was fun. I tipped my head to one side and monitor Carol... *what the hell?* What was that glow at the back of monitor Carol's crown? I reached up. Monitor Carol reached up. We fluffed the hair, a quick rearrangement to cover the patch of scalp. It remained. We tried again. No improvement. This was not fun. Barely coherent, we paid for our meal and slipped out of frame. At home that night and hardly stopping to strip off my coat before letting it fall to the floor, I ran to the bathroom, grabbed my hand mirror, turned my back to the mirror above the bathroom sink, and confirmed monitor Carol's testimony.

First thing the next morning I checked to see whether the patch had disappeared overnight (not at all) and last night's shock had calmed (not much). After breakfast, I Googled *hair loss women*. "Mistakenly thought to be a strictly male disease, women actually make up forty percent of American hair loss sufferers. Hair loss in women can be absolutely devastating for the sufferer's self-image and emotional well-being." [1]

Forty percent? That seemed a huge amount. I'd heard nowhere near as much about female hair loss as male. But I felt somewhat less alone — forty percent! And not only was I suddenly part of a crowd, I was not the only one reacting so strongly. "Most women keep their thinning hair a secret, often ache in silence [...] rarely discuss it with others." [2] The website for the American Hair Loss Association even called women's hair loss a serious, life-changing condition. [3]

Me and the sisterhood of balding women! Shouldn't membership make me feel better? Well ... no. I mean, maybe it should have, but it didn't. There was this niggling feeling of shame, though for what I didn't precisely know. I did get the irony, however. Where was the feminist who, having rejected retail marketing-hyped standards of female beauty most of her life, had been proud of aging gracefully? Accruing gray hairs had never bothered me: I'd earned every one. Wrinkles around my eyes? Laugh lines. Hint of jowls forming mid-way on my jaw line? Softening the look of my angular face. Age spots on my hands? Large freckles. But hair loss? Disaster, drama, *sturm und drang*.

§

I had hated my hair as soon as I was old enough — say, twelve — to realize that the straight, fine, fly-away hair that had looked so cute on my younger self was more like horrifying on my older self, especially as my forehead grew broader and my jaw grew squarer. The only way I could get body into it was to go at it with curling iron or hot rollers, and then hurriedly, before the curls sagged, plaster it with hair spray resembling wood lacquer more than beauty product.

As my hairline began to retreat in my thirties, it did so from the corners of my forehead. I adjusted by growing certain strands longer than others to cover the bare spots. It did not occur to me that this recession was a harbinger of things to come. I did not think of my strategy as a comb-over.

During my early fifties my hair thinned even more. I used a popular hair-loss remedy for almost a year. No new hair. I switched to an expensive, "scientific" remedy for another year. No new hair. Dismayed, I experimented with various hairstyles, all short, finally settling on one (the fateful one that monitor Carol wore) combing my hair forward to cover the sharply receding forehead corners. Had I picked up a hand mirror to check the back of my crown with all its hair swept forward, monitor Carol wouldn't have shocked me so. That said a lot about my level of denial.

§

I sulked in the car on the way to the wig shop the Saturday after meeting monitor Carol. Remembering my former rants about marketing and fashion industry standards of female beauty and how entrapped other women were to them, I was suddenly seeing exposed my own buy-in to at least one of those standards. I felt ashamed. I was no better than the women I'd felt better than.

Yet, I reminded myself, there was the forty percent. Balding women had good reason to feel shame, hair being such a mark of beauty and symbol of femininity. It was as though losing hair, like going bankrupt or being fired for cause or failing an important test, made us losers.

In an ambivalent haze and nervously glancing around to make sure no one was watching, I scooted in as Tim opened the wig shop door. The front windows were packed solid with mannequin heads wearing a riotous variety of wigs from long neon-blond to short curls sporting a green streak to wildly tousled raven black. They looked like they were meant for Halloween.

"I'm not going to buy one," I hissed at Tim, who had, with enviable nonchalance, outpaced my now-faltering steps. "I just want to try some on." He nodded, stopped to let me catch up, and we continued up the claustrophobically narrow aisle between shelves crammed with bewigged plastic heads. Two friendly looking Asian women stood near a cash register barely visible among the chaos of hair and Styrofoam faces and accessories.

"You want to try on wig?" asked one of the women. At my nod, she went on, "You ever wear wig before?"

"No, and I'm not ready to buy, just want to see what's available," I replied, feeling out of control and wishing passionately to be elsewhere. "I've lost a lot of hair."

"Oh," she said, stopping immediately and turning toward me with a concerned look. "Chemo?"

"Well, ah, no... " I stumbled over the words because it had just struck me that here I was, totally devastated about a bit of exposed scalp, in a place where a lot of women with far more valid reasons like cancer had been before me. "No, just... heredity." I sank into the chair she indicated, unable to look my mirrored self in the eye.

How lame was I?

But there was no time to process this new layer of shame. The nice lady put a net cap on my head, squashing my carefully curled and sprayed hair. "What you want? You like straight, curly, blonde? Brunette?"

I looked desperately at Tim, who reminded me we'd talked about finding one not too different from what grew (*or didn't*, I thought) naturally.

"Straight, brown or sorta auburn, maybe about chin length?" I said uncertainly as the feeling of being out of control fishtailed. Behind me on the shelf were wigs more modest, thankfully, than the ones in the front. She spun around and grabbed one. Holding it on hands with fingers spread wide, she angled it forward to settle the front on my forehead, then expertly eased the back in place, tugging at the ear tabs to center it.

It was glossy, straight yet full-looking hair with a nice curve to the chin-level ends. I didn't recognize myself. Helplessly, I glanced at Tim. He shook his head.

"How did you wear your hair before you started going, um, before it got so much thinner? Look for one like that," he said, making me frustrated at him for expecting me, in my current state, to remember that far back. As the wig was taken off my head, I asked the price. It was more than $500.

"Oh, no," I sputtered. "I'm in grad school. That's way too much."

The lady showed us a grouping on sale. As she picked one and smoothly put it on my head, I fought the urge to snatch it off and race out into the street. Had it not been for that ugly cap crushing my hair into what I knew was a stiff, flat mess, I would have done it, too. A dilemma of epic proportions: fierce desire to get the hell out of there slamming up against knowledge I couldn't run away because I'd look so awful doing it.

A succession of wigs—curly, straight, long, short, blonde, red—made their way to my head. I hated how they looked, shocked at the sight of all that hair on me. After a lifetime bemoaning my too-thin hair, I was now freaking out because the remedy looked so big.

How perverse was I?

Tim, seeing my quandary, pointed at a low shelf behind me. "This one is close to the color of your eyebrows," he said as the sales lady picked it up. "And it's like the style you had when we met."

He was right, yet I felt only dismay once it was in place. The wig, the first I thought might actually look half-way decent on me, seemed to call attention to itself. What if it either looked so fake I got laughed at or so good I got compliments? What if cancer-suffering women who *really* needed a wig felt contemptuous of me?

"She can cut," said the other woman, handing over a pair of scissors after Tim said he liked it and I said it looked like way too much hair. "Can make thinner."

But if I let her thin it, I'll have to buy it.

In an agony of indecision, I looked at the scissors. At Tim. At my reflection. At Tim. At the scissors. At my reflection. One thought broke through: *Either way, bald or wigged, I'll feel awful. Which is worse?*

"Make it thinner."

§

I take the wig home that day, just one week before the big public reveal: a long weekend at Goucher College where I'm studying for a master's degree in the low-residency non-fiction writing program. The shop woman had said to wear the wig every day for at least a week in order to get accustomed to it. I have six days until I have to be at school. Six days to get used to the feel of this thing on my head and the look of that woman in the mirror. Six days to act natural, if not feel natural, wearing it. Six days before exposing myself to people who have only seen me with short, wispy hair.

Sunday: I'm unwilling to admit to myself, let alone state for the record, exactly how much time I spend in the bathroom putting on and adjusting the wig. Turning my head from side to side, flipping and re-flipping the upturns at the back, sweeping and re-sweeping the curve of bangs at the front and studying my face as it makes every possible expression. Smiling, frowning. Looking intelligent, looking puzzled. Happy, sad. I raise my eyebrows, I purse my lips. Raise my eyebrows while pursing my lips. Some last, shredded vestige of dignity makes me stop just short of batting my eyelids at myself. Even after multiple adjustments, I'm unable to decide whether the wig looks better set higher on my forehead or lower.

It's a long day.

Monday: To my husband's surprise, I wear the wig to my morning dermatology appointment. "Considering that two days ago you were crying about needing it, I think you're courageous to wear it today." I am a lot closer to desperation than courage. Aside from questioning the wisdom of the expense when I'm saving to pay for school, I can't shake the worry that I either don't look good, or do look weird, in it. What if everyone else sees what I see: an aging woman who, in frenzied overcompensation, has substituted for pathetically too little with ridiculously too much?

It turns out to be a good decision, desperate or not. I ask the dermatologist before she begins the examination if she wants me to take off the wig. "That's a *wig*?" she says with what I interpret as genuine surprise. I immediately feel better, and so encouraged I stop at a Starbucks on the way home to drink tea, eat a scone and act natural.

Tuesday and Wednesday: More days at home wearing the wig and flirting with my mirror image. I decide I like it set lower on my forehead. Halfway through Wednesday morning, I realize I am about to spend a weekend with people who know me with short, thin hair. I panic. I send an email to six or seven school friends explaining about the wig and how insecure I feel so would they please not make a fuss when they see me. The message leaves out, at least explicitly, the stuff about vanity and shame. It demonstrates, to the readers if not to the writer, the futility of hoping to remain inconspicuous while trying to be attractive.

Back at the mirror, I like the way I look with the wig placed higher on my forehead.

Thursday: While packing before leaving for school in the afternoon, I check my email and find kind replies to mine of the day before. Once in my hotel room, I forsake the stuffed chair and my interesting book for the bathroom with its full-wall mirror. After deciding I like the wig set lower on my forehead, I leave for the café to meet a friend, one of the email recipients. She sits down, casts a quick glance over me and says, "It looks just like your hair. I don't know why you had to send that email." Her reaction bolsters my confidence and as I fall asleep I anticipate seeing everyone the next day with what might even be excitement.

Friday: Our first meeting isn't until three o'clock, which gives me time for a leisurely morning in front of the mirror and more vacillation on the higher/lower problem. At last, with a final twitch to push the wig higher, I leave for the meeting.

It's anti-climactic, really. One email recipient mouths the words *looks fabulous*, others manage a discreet nod or wink. Seeing no looks of pity or horror from the others in the room, I feel nominally better. That evening I enjoy the comfy chair and good book and, aside from one mirror session during which I decide the wig looks better lower on my forehead, am able to forget, for a while, the state of my scalp.

§

Maybe I don't look half-bad in this thing. This thought, popping up a week later when I'm at home fiddling with the wig's placement and brushing out the bangs, makes me wonder again at my vanity — overblown expectations of how much other people care how I look, inordinate amount of time logged at mirrors, and still-lurking shame about those bits of exposed scalp. I lower the brush and stare at my reflection. Have I always been this way?

There have been moments in my life I've been able to admit that I worry a lot about the way I look. But not the endless procession of shampoos and hair treatments and curling devices, the low self-esteem of bad hair days, even my envy of women with pretty hair had never seemed like real vanity to me. The treatments and products and hurt ego seemed more like survival techniques, practical in a world that assigns such importance to women's hair. Yet now, suddenly exhausted by the past few weeks' obsessions about the wig and how I look in it and what other people might think… I cannot help but name my vanity. And, now that I think about it, what about my own habit of looking at patchy-haired older women and assuming they are somehow, I don't know, lacking? Like they're too not-with-it or too old to pay attention and it was kind of cute, maybe, but in a way that engendered condescending amusement as opposed to, say, respect. It had never occurred to me to question these ageist judgments. Not until now, when I am the patchy-haired older woman.

I am a hairist.

I talk about this latent prejudice and overweening concern with something ultimately trivial with my friend and fellow-writer, Lauren, even though it's embarrassing because she has gone through cancer and chemo, hair loss and wigs. Her perspective is helpful. "But yours is just so permanent," she says. "When I lost the hair to chemo, I knew it would grow back and I'd put the wig away. You don't have that consolation."

The trauma, we agree, is not about mortality, but about how getting older affects our vanity.

§

I have survived the big reveal at school and come clean with my family by sending them wigged photos on my cell phone. Yet when my friend, David, is scheduled to come over for lunch, I vacillate about wearing the wig. How do wig-wearers manage in-house guests? And David, honest to a fault, will be the acid test. He blurts the most honest things ever said to me without rancor, like *wow, you look terrible in that photo,* or *don't talk like that, you sound weird,* in the same easy tone he would use to discuss weather.

But we live near one another and have friends in common, and what would I do if we were to meet in public, me with my wig that he's never seen and he with his forthrightness?

Just before he arrives for lunch, I decide upon a compromise: I'll host him *sans* wig but make sure to mention it. When, over the salad and biscuits, I work up the nerve to tell him, he asks to see it. I bring it out draped over one fist like the pelt of some urban subspecies of mink. "Well that doesn't tell me anything," he says. "You have to put it on." Thinking that refusing will only cause a fuss, I retreat to the bathroom mirror. *Just wear it like it's hot,* I tell myself somewhat ridiculously and not at all originally. I put the wig on, fiddling with the bangs and the wisps around my face and the flips at the back and the shape of the left side and the shape of the top and the shape of the right side. I decide I like it higher on my forehead.

David gazes steadily at me as I return and sit down. I try not to feel self-conscious, but it gets awkward the longer he remains quiet. In fact, it's unnerving, this silence from my friend who is never at a loss for words. Suddenly the damn wig is itching the hell out of my head. I'm on the verge of screaming, flinging off the wig and raking frantic fingernails across my scalp when he finally speaks.

"You're wearing it too high on your forehead."

§

A year has gone by, and I've wrenched myself from the mirror habit. Mostly. With the time freed up I worry about things like what my friends and family *really* think of the wig. Does the mailman notice? The pharmacist? Should I wear it to walk my dog? Workout?

All the while, my inner feminist is trying to get my attention. I know she's there. I believe she wants me to see how low I've sunk. And I'll pay attention to her just as soon as I'm satisfied with the look of these curvy wisps I've combed forward toward my cheekbones.

---

[1]From the website of The American Hair Loss Association, www.americanhairloss.org/women_hair_loss
[2]ibid
[3]"Women's Hair Loss: Breaking the Silence and Seeking Solutions" Dr. Ronald L. Moy, January 4, 2013, www.Lifeafter50.com

Personal Training
Patty Somlo

The black rubber tongue of the treadmill stretches across a metal frame, before rolling to a place my feet can't reach. Adam waits on the machine next to me, as I step one clean white athletic shoe in front of the other. Glancing out the corner of my eye, I notice his hair that's shiny as squid's ink has been cut short, and I wonder if I should tell him it looks nice.

It's been several weeks since Adam and I first met. That day, with almost nothing said, Adam led me to a back office and ordered me to step up on the scale.

"Can I take my shoes off first?" I pleaded.

"No," Adam said, without a single missed breath.

The numbers came up huge and red. Like my clothes shopping bills, the total was a great deal higher than I'd expected.

If seeing the numbers hadn't been disturbing enough, Adam added a second insult by announcing the results.

"Now we have something to start with," he added gaily, as if he might toss the pounds into the air and watch them dissolve.

We moved onto measurements. After stretching the tape measure around my bust, waist and hips, Adam was kind enough to keep the numbers to himself.

The final humiliation came when he collected several inches of my skin between his fingers and pinched it with a large clip.

Once Adam was done, he knew more about me than Dr. Matsumura, who checks me out once a year. He led me to the exercise room and gestured for me to take a seat. Surrounded by ropes, nooses and bars, Adam stared at the numbers he'd written on a sheet and then gave me his unvarnished opinion.

"Your goal should be to lose twenty pounds," he said. "We'll meet for an hour twice a week."

§

At this point, I feel like a battle-scarred vet. The depression I dove into, after learning the facts about my fat, seems like a long-forgotten dream. Being good at what he does, Adam must have known he needed to slap the numbers across my face, to scare me away from the table and over to lifting weights.

It worked. Before I'd recovered, Adam let the next blow fall. He handed me several sheets describing the meals I was allowed to eat. Unlike my weight and body fat, the calories I was permitted were shockingly low.

Today, Adam leads me over to a machine I would avoid on my own. Round black plates hang from bars on the back, each plate successively larger and thicker than the next. He lifts off the banquet-size plates, moving them to the rear, and slides two delicate dishes perfect for petit fours onto the shiny metal bars in front.

I watch as he sits down and demonstrates what I'm to do next. My mind tries to catalogue each posture—elbows out, shoulders down, head back.

We move back and forth between two of these machines, one of which pulls, another of which pushes. I do well on the pull machine, so Adam adds on heavier weights. The push machine is another matter, especially since I'm moving one arm at a time. Being right-handed, my left arm acts like a spoiled rich lady who has deeded the heavy lifting to the hired help. I'm having trouble getting my left arm through the second set of reps, and Adam helps by giving my elbow a soft shove. Even though I've relied on his help, Adam assures me I've done a good job.

§

On the first visit my husband Richard and I made to this club, the tour took several hours. Our guide, a young Asian man, acted excessively interested in us. I didn't want to admit that the place frightened me, with machines lined up one after the next, and what seemed like hundreds of hard-breathing, sweating bodies pumping, jogging, jiggling and bouncing up and down on each one. Music pounded over the click and whir of the equipment. TVs blinked and flickered in every direction I looked.

Richard, who's been hefting weights the past year, was thrilled, especially once we stepped into the holy sanctuary of testosterone — the free weight room. At that moment, he turned to me and grinned.

"They have everything," he said, his eyes shimmering, as if he'd just seen God.

Another fast-talking young man convinced me to sign up for personal training, making sure I understood that the low-price deal was only going to last another day. I was also easy to reel in, weakened by middle-age bulge and at least three failed attempts to get rid of it. I'd cut down my eating, or at least that's what I thought, and upped my exercise, to no effect. Some days I worried that my efforts might be causing me to gain even more weight.

§

I wonder what Adam is thinking, as he watches me struggle to lift five pounds with my left arm or hold myself up above the blue mat using my abdominals, the side of my foot and one arm in contact with the ground, a feat lifted out of the Marine Corps' basic training manual. Adam's attention hardly ever strays from me. He's constantly checking my posture and technique, prodding me to go higher or lower, and keep my head back, elbow up, abs tucked. I'm unaccustomed to being the one that matters, the woman constantly on someone else's mind, and find it both disconcerting and delightful. There's an odd intimacy to our relationship, as Adam presses my shoulders with his fingertips or directs me to lie down sideways facing him while he demonstrates some new technique.

At the same time, we are not close at all. I don't know where he lives or what he does in his spare time. I don't know if he's married. I've never seen what he looks like in street clothes. When we meet, he's always wearing the certified personal trainer's uniform—black, knee-length shorts and a T-shirt that's bright red.

Kind and serious as he seems, I believe that Adam has a wilder side. A long blue tattoo runs the length of his left leg, terminating along his well-muscled calf. Another tattoo graces his upper arm, which I peek at when his shirt momentarily slides up. Dark enough to be dyed, his hair is cut in a spiky style. His ears are pierced, though I've never seen earrings dangling there.

Because we spend several hours together each week, I want to get to know Adam better and for him to know me. At the same time, I am completely out of touch with Adam's generation. I can't figure out how old he might be. If I had a son, I suspect he would be Adam's age.

I'm easy prey for making more out of relationships. Other than Richard, I don't have a single close friend. I'm making more of the personal part of the training than I should. I'm tempted to tell Adam some detail about myself, as he waits on the treadmill next to me while I warm up. After I leave the session exhausted and damp from sweat, I have a conversation with Adam in my head.

§

When I met Richard years ago, on an Indian summer afternoon in San Francisco that felt magical because the fog hadn't appeared for days, I was slender as a long-distance runner. One of the things Richard found attractive about me were the prominent bones below my neck that formed a delicate vee. That year, I sometimes got dressed up in short, tight dresses and heels, to go out with Richard to dinner or dancing or to watch the ballet. At times when we walked through the city, Richard would comment that a man we just passed had been staring at me.

The signs first appeared below my temples, in hair-thin lines that refused to leave, even once I quit squinting. After that, my face slowly shifted, like unstable land inching its way downhill. Parentheses started on each side above my mouth, but were soon joined by a matching pair underneath. Then all hell broke loose after that.

While having my hair cut one day, I noticed

what appeared to be a double chin. Naturally, I assumed that my chair was raised up, so the mirror had given me a distorted reflection from underneath. But the longer I looked, the more the truth became clear. The skin under my chin had now decided to droop.

Like the lines, the weight arrived unexpectedly. One day, I looked like a dancer, with legs and hips onto which tight knit pants loved to cling. The next moment, I was fat. Suddenly, the tops of my inner thighs desperately reached for one another, any time I slipped on a pair of pants. My hips had grown convenient little hooks my arms got caught on as I walked. The weight forced me to bury myself under long loose tops. With the fat and extra material, I moved through the city feeling like a person packed in Styrofoam.

Instead of giving me an admiring eye, men now let me step onto the bus first. Bus drivers lowered the entry platform for me, as if I'd pole-vaulted from middle age to senility. From shop windows, short skirts and slim belted sweaters leered, taunting me with the grim news that my chance to wear cute clothes had come and gone. I even started to hate going on vacation in Hawaii, having to subject myself to long lines of beautiful bodies on the beach, while I stretched across the sand, looking like a stranded seal.

§

This morning as I'm drying my hair, I notice a pair of tender bones peeking out below my neck. The sight causes me to tremble and worry that if I look too long, they might disappear. Later, I walk upstairs and pull a faded pair of denim shorts out of the drawer. Luckily, I snatched this pair from the Goodwill donation bag, where they'd been tossed when I could barely yank them on. Now, they almost fit.

This must be what it's like to go under the knife, starting out one morning droopy and old, and a few weeks later when the bandages come off, seeing your face as it was when you were young. Only you're not.

And that's what has gotten me feeling confused. Even though I'm beginning to emerge like a wet butterfly from my round cocoon, I am not ever going to be reborn young.

Could the fat have been cushioning me from a painful fall, as my newly thin body comes crashing against the middle-aged floor of life? Might I have grown plump, so I'd never again see a man's head turn as I walked?

§

Tonight I stand in front of the Testosterone Temple's wall of mirrors, practicing a move I haven't done before. The woman reflected back to me balances on her left leg, with her right leg lifted and tucked. When she thinks she might be steady, she bends her left knee and reaches her right hand to the foot on the ground. It's an awkward exercise that keeps me wobbling from side to side, prepared at any moment to topple down.

But after a time, I'm no longer thinking about what to do next. Surprisingly, my body keeps holding me up. It's as if some strange power has decided to surge up my leg from the floor, each time I kneel down.

I may not get stares from anyone here in the T Temple tonight. But the woman in the mirror suddenly flashes me a sly grin. I know that she and I are thinking a similar thought — that my ability to go down is what has given me this surging energy to keep moving ever so defiantly back up.

The Ugly Business of Getting Old
Falconhead

"It wouldn't happen to us," we told ourselves.

But how wrong we were. Perhaps we shouldn't have taken notice of it. Shouldn't have let the thought enter our minds, for, in doing so, we woke it, summoned it, let the poison in.

We wore black then, as did all our friends, and never took to anything else. We blackened our eyes, our hair. Our hearts. The boys wore trench coats — their collars turned up, their hair shaved & dyed — and the girls wore strange earrings & black stockings beneath it all.

The girls were different creatures from the boys. They were more secretive (as they still are, I suppose), and the boys hadn't the heads to know that girls knew better than them. Or did they?

Did they know that when the girls weren't around, the boys — some in makeup, some in Mohawks — kissed one another? Did they know not to play Russian roulette because doing so puts a bullet through the skull? Did they know not to get a job, not to let one's parents die, and not to fall in love? Because doing so stirs it, angers it, lets it into the blood where it thickens, hardens, and makes one tired—complacent. No, I suppose they didn't know either.

But we knew, didn't we? Us two… We made a vow, that night. And kept it. A vow never to grow old, never become our parents, our fears. And though we made the vow, it wasn't so much aging we feared but rather the loss of self. Yes, that self, which we had fought our parents to become—their rules, the unobserved simplicity in which they lived their lives, made their money, raised their children only to, horror of horrors, grow old.

Then the years passed…

And the last I heard what's-her-name got married, had a child, lived simply, but contentedly, I suppose. Then, the last I heard of you, after my father died, was that you had gotten a job. But never anything else. You hadn't changed—so you were safe, only half your age because of it. You never married—you're still the girl I once knew.

I miss that girl. I miss those times. For anything was believable then, everything was possible.

Well, I'm just writing to tell you that I'm still young, that I still write, but that I've found someone, that I've fallen in love (you know, like what's-her-name did) and that we talk of marriage. Yes, of getting married one day. And we're looking for a home of our own. But I promise you—I'll never get old. Yes, I promise that, well, if you promise to come and visit. Come and tell me all about the things you're doing, and whom it is you're seeing these days. Yes, come and visit soon, there's someone I love whom I want you to meet. And when you do, promise me you'll be in black. That you'll wear strange earrings, and that you'll tell me, as we stay up late talking about all those untold nights, if you knew when I too had kissed other boys.

Pilly
Dustin Hyman

My grandma Nini had some good pills, but her roommate, Mrs. Larsen, she had a fucking goldmine. I heard them rattling around one day as she searched for the perfect pair of "stockings" to match her faded yellow nightgown. When Mrs. Larsen went to the bathroom, I slowly opened the drawer. *Holy fuck.* She had Klonopin for anxiety, Vicodin for pain, Lunesta to sleep, and Provigil to stay awake. She had a pill for everything…except rosacea, halitosis, and loneliness. I started visiting them every Friday.

§

I was watching TV with my grandma when Mrs. Larsen died. She sat up in her bed and announced: "I need to go." I thought she had a bathroom emergency, but she just closed her eyes and left. She actually did poop her pants — so I'll never know if she was prophesying her own death, or, if she was simply being candid about a bowel movement.

§

I waited in the cafeteria for things to calm down. It smelt like warm piss and muffins. When all was calm again, I snuck back into their room. Grandma Nini was asleep, so I slowly opened Mrs. Larsen's sock drawer and began transferring pills into my backpack. When I turned to leave, Nini was staring at me.

"What are you doing, Billy?"

"I need these," I said.

"Suicide?" she asked.

"I owe a kid some money." I had a cocaine habit.

"So what are the pills for?" she asked.

"Nini, these pills are worth like 200 bucks."

She grabbed the cup beside her and took a sip of warm milk.

"I want half," she said.

"For what?" I asked.

"I need better medicine," she said.

"What kind of medicine?" I asked.

"You don't listen to anything I say do you, Billy?"

Grandma Nini had diabetes and something else. She wouldn't let me leave until I promised her half the cash. I sold the pills and made 600 bucks. When I gave Nini her cut, she had more pills for me. A lot more.

"Where did you get all these?" I asked.

"Look around you," she said. "People are dying around here, kid."

I scanned the cafeteria. Half the old folks were on motorized carts. Some people had oxygen tanks. Everyone had pills out to take with their turkey-meatloaf and Jell-O. Each day they swallowed ten thousand dollars' worth of medication. They drank powdered iced-tea. If the doctors prescribed it, they'd swallow arsenic. To say they were vulnerable wouldn't make sense—they had no defense.

"Don't even think about it," she said. "I'd rat you out, kiddo."

§

I made $1,100 on the new pills and gave Nini 300 bucks. She didn't really show it, but I could tell she was happy. She looked younger, too.

§

My mom was always snooping around my room, so I kept the cash I was making locked up in my truck. I was doing good business until I started swallowing the pills. It was never a problem before because I couldn't afford the good pills. But when I had them for free, I got addicted to strange combos. Morning pills, afternoon pills, party pills. People at school started calling me Pilly. My favorite pills targeted anxiety, but painkillers were good too—combining them worked best. Grandma Nini noticed me changing.

"Why don't you lay off the medications?" she

asked.

"I'll stop when you stop," I said.

"Billy," she said. "Let's go for a drive."

"I just drove here to see you."

"No," she said. "You drove here for these."

She handed me a plastic bag. I kissed her on the cheek and left.

§

I gave her 500 bucks a week later. She didn't even count the money. She just looked at me and started crying.

"You look like a zombie, Billy."

"So do you," I said.

"I'm ninety two years old. What's your excuse?"

"Where are they?" I asked.

"It's over," she said.

"Why?" I asked.

"Because of your appearance," she said.

I stood to leave.

"Don't you wanna go for a drive?" she asked.

"I'll see you next Friday," I said.

"Don't come back until you're better," she said.

§

I was back Friday morning, before school. Grandma Nini saw me and rolled her eyes.

"Jesus," she said. "I knew it."

"I'm just here to talk," I said.

"Really?" she asked.

"Yeah, but if you have more pills…I'll sell them for you."

"There are no more pills," she said.

I got up and began opening drawers.

"Get out of here, Billy!"

I couldn't find any pills in her room, but Mr. Monteath had some, so did Mrs. Pearson. I swallowed three lorazepam and buckled in. I didn't get far. The cops pulled me over before I got to school. They searched my backpack and found little pill bottles with other people's names on them. I was busted, sabotaged by Grandma Nini. They laid all my shit out on the hood of their squad car and started shaming me. They always do that. That's when I saw them. Grandma Nini was on Mr. Monteath's motorized chair, sitting on his lap. It took about five minutes for them to finally reach us. Mr. Monteath killed Japs in WWII. He was excited talking with the cops. When they cuffed me, Grandma Nini grabbed my keys. I don't know where she was going—but she left in a hurry. It's been nine years.

The Visit
Anthony Bain

I think it is fair to say that for the longest time I had been shirking my family responsibilities. My self-inflicted exile from my own family had gotten to the point where communication was strained and distant. I had cocooned myself in the London suburbs and when the phone began to ring, little did I know that my isolation bubble was about to pop.

"Finally," said my sister Faye with an exasperated voice that was her calling card. "I've been trying to get ahold of you for days."

Faye's voice seemed tense, even more strained than usual. I could imagine her there, as pale as snow, her eyes desperately darting around the room. She was never one for telephone small talk; she always went straight to the nub of whatever was bothering her.

"If you can engage your brain for a moment," she said, grinding her teeth, which was her way of hiding her constant frustration, "I'd like to remind you that we are flying out to Sardinia tomorrow; you agreed to take Dad for two weeks."

Over an awkward dinner some months ago, I had agreed, without thinking, to look after him while she took her family on their yearly summer holidays.

"I'll bring him by first thing tomorrow morning. Did you get the list I sent you?"

Then I remembered the email she had sent over a couple of weeks ago, the "dos and don'ts of looking after our father" — a comprehensive guide to his behavioral traits that had become the norm, things that would make your hair stand on end.

The email sat read but without a reply in my inbox, like most of Faye's email rants, demanding my time and my sanity. To be honest, I thought she'd given up sending them.

The next day, Faye arrived with my father. She brought a faded child's rucksack full of clothes and videotapes. He stood in the doorway vacantly looking out at a dog walker's park across the street. Then he peered into the house looking straight past me. He didn't seem to recognize the house, a house that had once belonged to him or his son, his only son.

"Give him ten minutes," said Faye with a hint of frustration that she reserved just for me.

"Faye, Faye, Faye!" he said like a child trying to draw his mother's attention. "What is that person over there doing?" He pointed to a traffic warden gliding in and out of parked cars.

"How I am supposed to know?" she fired

back at him impatiently. I sensed she was eager to get out the door.

Faye quickly checked the room he would be staying in, a recently converted utility room on the ground floor of our two-story semidetached house like a prison warden inspecting a cell. She began to bark orders at me. "He likes to listen to audio books at night. Did you get my message to get a cassette player?" She handed me a stack of old comedy cassette tapes from the rucksack. "He likes to listen to *Hancock's Half Hour* at night; it helps him sleep. Did you read the email I sent you?"

Faye didn't wait for a reply. She said she had a plane to catch.

I stood in the hallway and watched him stare out at nothing, his eyes seeing things that his brain could not understand, his brain receiving messages his eyes could no longer see. I didn't relish the idea of becoming old myself; perhaps eighty was a good age to take leave of one's senses.

"Why don't you come in, Dad?"

"I'm fine out here," he replied. "What's that drilling sound?"

"Road works, Dad. Welcome to London."

The local supermarket was thankfully quiet when we arrived with the simple yet problem-filled mission of getting our dinner for the evening.

"Don't you do monthly shopping?" asked my father as we walked through the door. "Faye does."

He began to sort through mangy bags of fruit on display like an exasperated gardener, sifting through bagged pineapple and mango cubes browning under the insufficient power of the refrigeration units. "I should complain," he began saying over and over. "I should speak to the manager."

I grabbed the bare essentials: eggs, bread, milk and cereals, things that are completely absent in my house. My busy work life meant that I seldom ate at home. My kitchen only served for making espressos and eating takeaways.

At the checkout, a shop attendant tapped me on the shoulder. "Does he belong to you?" She pointed to my father, somewhere up aisle seven in mid-conversation with a loaf of bread.

That evening I made my father eggs and bacon on toast for dinner while we watched reruns of long dead British sitcoms from a worn VHS tape.

During the evening he didn't speak directly to me, but let out great guffaws of laughter. I watched him from the kitchen while I made dinner. He would randomly call out for Faye like a child missing its mother, only to realize with a heavy sigh that she wasn't there.

After the VHS tape had finally ground to a halt, I took him to bed, for my sake more than his. I felt exhausted just watching him.

"I can't sleep without listening to *Hancock's Half Hour*," he said. "Where are my pajamas?"

He looked at me bewildered, waiting for me do something. I went to the loft space and began digging through boxes. After a while I eventually found an old Fisher-Price cassette player and some batteries. My father was unusually quiet as I came back downstairs; I caught a glimpse of him standing in the living room staring into space, his mind looped into some past episode of his conscientious life.

That night I couldn't sleep, my mind reeling in dread, my ear tuned to the faint drone of the cassette tape in play. Finally it stopped and the play button clicked back into place. A silence ensued as I listened for movement. Just as I was beginning to drift off to sleep, a sudden wailing began to sound.

Like a shot, the wailing brought me downstairs, with the echo of my father's desperate cries rebounding off the walls of the house.

"Father," I said through the door. "Are you okay?"

"I need the bathroom," he said, his voice slipping. I could hear him stumbling around the room like a confused drunk. I opened the door and grabbed him just as he was about to fall head first into the bedroom cupboard. "Get off me," he screamed. "I don't know you."

I let go of him and he slumped to the floor. On every level he was right; he didn't know me. I was the absent son, disconnected from what was left of my family. Living in exile in a leafy London suburb, God only knows what they thought of me.

I could hear the neighbors stirring as my father continued to shriek. I had to do something quickly. I had to meet him at his level, get into his mind. I had to stop him somehow, anyhow.

"Dad," I said, picking him up from the floor. His head rolled around as if disconnected from his neck. "What was the Monty Python sketch we used to watch?"

He looked at me side on. "What?" he said, his mind engaging.

"The Spanish Inquisition," I said. "Remember that?" I lifted him onto the bed. "Hah! Nobody expects the Spanish Inquisition," I said, putting on a ridiculous voice. "Their chief weapon is surprise," I bellowed. "Fear and surprise."

Monty Python was the last thing I remember watching with him, sometime around Christmas, a thousand years before.

Dad's composure seemed to change; he began to snigger like a schoolboy. The neighbors began to bang the walls. I took my father to the bathroom and then to bed. I lay down beside him for a while and began to reel off random Monty Python quotes off the top of my head, acting them out, changing my voice to suit the different characters. My father laughed until he cried and then he laughed some more; then miraculously he slept.

The next day I left to him to his VHS collection while I caught up with some work from my office at home. Just as I was on the phone to a client I saw him meandering about in the garden, peering over the fence into the neighbor's garden with a frequency that was beginning to worry me.

"What are you doing?" I said, trying to hide the irritability in my voice.

"You have cats in your garden," he said. I looked around the garden. There were no cats. I lived in an area of London where nighttime creatures were frequent; my neighbors left food out for them.

"I don't like cats," he added. "They leave droppings all over the place."

He stabbed a yellowing finger towards the neighbor's garden. "This is not good." For a moment I saw a faint glimmer of the man he once was, a company director, a leader in his field.

Again in desperation, I reached into our history and brought out something to diffuse the situation. "Remember that Monty Python sketch about the parrot?" I said unconvincingly, trying to diffuse him.

"What are you going to do about these cats?"

he said, cutting me off.

"They're just cats," I said shrugging my shoulders. "What harm can they do?"

"They use your garden as a toilet."

To my horror he produced a plastic bag full of animal droppings that he had been hiding behind his back. He must have spent the morning collecting them. With the evidence dangling before my face, I was completely shocked and totally lost for words.

He grunted at me and shrugged his shoulders. "Do something," he said, not hiding the aggressive tone of his voice. A flicker of my childhood still reflected in his stare, the man whom I had hidden from under the stairs on my tenth birthday had made a sudden and unexpected return. He was scolding me.

"Okay," I said. I couldn't see any easy way out of this situation. My father is known for stubbornness to the point of no return.

"Let's do something about it," I replied, my brain desperately searching for a way to placate him.

That evening I set out two deck chairs on the garden lawn. After some time rummaging through the attic, I found two heavy-duty florescent yellow water pistols and some old water balloons from some long-lost childhood summer party. I set up a halogen lamp that lit up the forgotten corners of my garden. For good measure I gave my father an old plastic U.S.

Army helmet that I had been given for my tenth birthday. I had painted three stars on it. He wore it like George Patton.

That night we laid an ambush for every cat and urban nighttime creature of West London that frequented my garden to empty their bowels, hitting them with a wall of water that took them completely by surprise, sending them running for cover. That night we reclaimed my garden and set up a dishcloth flag proclaiming it a wildlife-free territory; that evening we laughed until we cried, and then we laughed some more.

In the Cooling Twilight
Ed Meek

Thirty — the promise of a decade of loneliness,
a thinning list of single men to know, a thinning
briefcase of enthusiasm, thinning hair... so we
drove on toward death in the cooling twilight.
(*The Great Gatsby*)

I remember thirty; I was young then. I wasn't
even married. I had girlfriends. I drank to excess
and stayed up late. Weekends I played
basketball with teenagers. What was Fitzgerald
talking about? He was twenty-seven when he
wrote those lines. He was just guessing. He
went on to live to the ripe old age of forty-four
when his excesses caught up with him. I've just
turned sixty. By the time you're sixty you've
come face to face with fate. For my midlife crises
I took a leave of absence a few years ago from
my day job teaching at a small liberal arts
college to take a stab at my lifelong dream of
writing. After six months of life as a starving
artist, I picked up a job teaching at a private

high school.

My sister-in-law is sixty. She just retired from her job as head of human resources at a major accounting firm. She's in search of more satisfying, less time-consuming work. She's been volunteering in a women's prison and taking courses in religious studies. Like many sixty-year-olds, she wants to change her fate.

At forty you are middle-aged. What are you at sixty? Old? Not quite yet. This is not "The End" Jim Morrison sang about but the end looms, somewhere off in the distance. It looks closer than it is, like a full moon behind the trees on a clear night. It makes you consider what you are doing, how you are spending your time. If you are sick of your job, you are already planning on what you can do when you retire. If there's something else you've always wanted to do, this could be your chance to do it. This could be your final chance to start your own business. If you're unhappily married, you're ready to get a divorce. If you hate your car, you're going to trade it in for the convertible, or the jeep, or the bicycle.

At sixty we drive on toward death in the cooling twilight. It won't be long until we "rage, rage against the dying of the light." But that's because our night vision is going. What else? We need reading glasses. We have injuries that never entirely heal, phantom pains in damp weather, remaining hair turning gray, slow thinking and slower reactions, the inability to focus on multiple tasks, waning sex drive, memory loss. No wonder males over fifty commit suicide more than any other group.

Women attempt it more but men are more successful. Women favor pills. They'd rather be discovered. Guys go for guns. Say you decide you can't change your fate, that the bed you've made is a mess. You can't sleep in it, never mind lie in it. The walls of the room are closing in, the air unfit to breath and the living? Better off without you. So you take out the revolver you keep locked up downstairs and place the barrel against your temple. One more reason not to keep a gun in the house...

By sixty you are who you are. Americans are obsessed with identity. Adolescents work overtime to establish their individuality. They rely heavily on appearance. They need piercings and tattoos and orange hair to distinguish their tribe. We become who we are in our thirties and forties; by sixty, we are there. This means that when you are sixty there is no more lying. I don't mean lying to others but lying to yourself. Bill Clinton knows that he is rake. He's trying to make up for it by helping others, especially Hillary.

Numbers say those of us in our sixties will witness the death of one, or even both of our parents soon. My father is mid-eighties. My mother died last year of heart failure. My wife's parents have both passed away. Just staying healthy has become a challenge. One brother-in-law has diabetes, another has chronic back pain from lymphoma. My sister never fully recovered from breast cancer. My wife was diagnosed with leukemia last fall. She was treated with chemo and it is in remission, thank God.

Isn't that a good reason to begin living a healthier life? To start, you could cut down on the booze. You can't drink anymore anyway. More than three drinks and you can't sleep. You can't drink and drive. If you do you may forget to turn your lights on. Since you can't see as well at night, you drive too slowly or you take the exit too fast and let me tell you something, there is nothing more embarrassing than getting pulled over for drinking and driving at this stage in life. I got pulled over last year when I had four beers (watching the NCAA play-offs with a friend at a local bar). I wasn't drunk but the cop (who couldn't have been more than twelve years old) wouldn't believe me. He had my car towed. It was only after I took a breathalyzer at the station that they let me go. I slunk home and paid eighty bucks to retrieve my car the next morning.

You could step up the exercise. You see a lot of people over sixty running and playing tennis and going to the gym. One in four of us exercise regularly, a figure that has remained constant over the last two decades. I run three or four times a week. I ran a marathon last spring but I had to walk the last six miles. It took me four and a half hours. If I were running to warn the

Athenians, the city would be under siege by the time I got there. I also lift weights for twenty minutes two or three days a week. I try to do this around five in the afternoon but if I am tired or don't feel like it, I skip it and have a beer instead.

A few years ago on a whim I decided to try snowboarding under the impression that it would be easier on my knees than skiing. It turns out that snowboarding is easier on the knees and is a lot of fun. There are, however, a couple of minor drawbacks. For one thing, you fall all the time. Where it is okay to fall when you are ten, twenty, even thirty, a fall at sixty can result in nagging injuries. I sprained my wrist on New Year's Day and it was two months before I could lift weights again. And although snowboarding is easier on the knees, it's harder on the back. I had to be taken down the mountain on a rescue sled last winter when my back went out. It was kind of fun but really embarrassing.

The other problem is not with snowboarding itself but with what it brings to light and that is: the fear. Don't tell anyone about this because it is a secret among guys, but the fear begins to sneak up on you in your forties and by the time you're sixty, it has taken up residence in your house. I know because fifteen years ago, I painted my house. I bought a nice twenty-eight-foot fiberglass ladder so I could reach the eaves. I used to work as a painter in summers when I was in college and I know what I'm doing, but whenever I climbed up on that ladder I had to psych myself up. I'd get nervous up there. I could see the headlines: Man Plunges to Death While Painting House. Man Blown Off Ladder. Or worse: Man Rescued From Ladder by Local Fire Department.

The other problem with snowboarding is that snowboarders do jumps. The little jumps, one or two feet high are fine but my son, who is twenty, likes to do the big jumps, the ten and fifteen footers which are giant white cliffs of snow created by the deranged men who groom the slopes at night. In my mind's eye I can make these jumps. I was a gymnast in high school, but when I try them now, I often fall down on purpose while approaching takeoff. If I happen to make the jump I usually fall afterward in a wimpy attempt to slow down.

Better I fall than my son. If anything happens to him I may start weeping. I've become very emotional, very sensitive. I often find myself choking up watching television shows or movies or reading novels. Newspaper stories can also make me lose it. Old photos? Forget about it. In short, I've become sentimental. Of course, this is better than being the callous, devil-may-care fool I was in my twenties but it is a bit unnerving.

Okay I'm being disingenuous. For one thing, it's much better than I thought it would be. I am, after all, able to run (I ran a 1:48 half-marathon last fall); I do lift weights, snowboard, and enjoy sex. I also know what's good in wine, food, cigars, books, magazines, movies. And early mornings I seem to be able to see more clearly than ever how the light strikes the trees, illuminates the grass and infiltrates the water. The sunsets seem to be getting better, and I don't mind hearing the song sparrow outside my window at five a.m. because I'm already awake anyway. I guess you could call turning sixty a mixed bag, which is better than being an old bag.

Perhaps the Russians had the right idea. In Chekhov's plays, a man of sixty is in his prime — at the top of his career — ready to settle down and marry. I've read personals that say: Sixty and fabulous. Some older women do look great. There's Cher Surgery, Goldie-still-cute-Hawn, Susan-still-sexy-Sarandon.

Maybe science will rescue us. Bill Nye was right when he claimed, "science rules." Science now operates outside anyone's control. That could be good news for us in terms of longevity, replacement parts, memory enhancement and cures for many of the diseases that plague person-kind. Evidently we'll leave the next generation to deal with implanting computer chips, genetic manipulation, cyborgs and clone clans. I'm against anything that makes us less human, but in another thirty years when my son will be dealing with those changes, I won't have anything to say about it. I'll be enjoying the big sleep.

The Wedding
Niles Reddick

Having been married for twenty years and knowing it's not a daily cakewalk, I'm leery about attending weddings, particularly when those getting married have been married before, but I went because I felt like I should and I wanted to be supportive and positive. The drive was only about half an hour, but the first question my wife asked was: "Do you think we should have brought a gift?"

"A gift?"

"Yeah."

"Do you get gifts every time you get married?"

"I don't know," she said.

"Hell, as many times as he's been married, he ought to have a warehouse full. I mean this is his fifth. Her third." She shook her head while I laughed at my own sarcasm. I added, "Hey, maybe we should get them a gift certificate to e-harmony or to a divorce attorney." She smirked. I figured given their track record, it seemed reasonable to assume they'd have yet another go at it.

When we pulled in, there were pastel signs planted in the ground, leading us to the old plantation house on Gator Pond, a pond covering over a thousand acres, chock-full of lily pads, turtles, moccasins, and alligators. Occasionally, one would get word of a high school senior taking a dare and swimming in there among the gators, but people had disappeared through the years, boats found empty and floating willy-nilly through the swamp being propelled by wind and currents. Fishermen usually avoided the banks because of stories of gators charging up banks to take unsuspecting prey, drag them in, roll them and store them in their underwater burrows.

Once parked, we walked through the grass, my wife's heels sinking into the moist ground, and found our way to the groom's side of folding chairs, where handheld fans, same pastel colors, aided in gnat control. The metal arbor with plastic flowers was the altar, and once the minister and groom had arrived, they stood off-center, askew. The bride, astoundingly, wore a long white dress, and I wondered if it was a new one or one from the two previous weddings. For whatever reason, I thought white was reserved for the first wedding and that long dresses were reserved for evening ceremonies. He, on the other hand, looked like a pimp in a white linen suit, white pointed patent leather shoes, a straw fedora.

The minister droned on about the holiness of matrimony, and I wondered if he knew about the six marriages between them. He talked about marriage being for life, and I wondered if the logic was that each marriage was considered a different life. He talked about them becoming one and I wondered if that meant their checking accounts and assets, since my friend's fourth seemed to have drained him better than the embalmer at the funeral home would. At least, it wasn't permanent and he recovered.

When they read their vows, I rolled my eyes at the silliness and saw a gator at the edge of the pond, sunning. I imagined the gator racing toward them, snatching one of them, and dragging him or her to the pond, clawing dirt, being pulled under, rolled, and stored for a later supper in the burrow deep below the surface. I imagined people screaming for help, all the sounds echoing across the pond, and falling on deaf ears. By the time I whacked myself in the face with the fan, they were kissing, and a relative yelled, "Yeehaw, go for it cousin!" As they walked up the isle together, a loner stood up and broke into song, a tenor squeaking out a redneck love song, and I changed my mind. I wanted the gator to take him under.

The reception was nice, lots of hors d'oeuvres, good cake, and plenty to drink, and I wished the couple well by toasting them and wondered how many of their relatives prayed this wedding took and would be the last. I left full and felt I'd done my part, and on the drive home, my wife asked, "What'd you think?"

"Waste of money. They should've gone to the courthouse."

"I thought it was nice."

"I just hope this lasts."

"Me, too."

Seven Words
Meneese Wall

"What an interesting yellow," Mother said, just two weeks before she died.

"It's called Amber Flush," I noted as I replaced last week's prickly pink offering. Each week, I brought a beautiful, plump rose to brighten her bedside table — so many I could no longer smell them, and my taste buds began to cower each time I reached for a florist's shop door. She'd been ill for months.

Fancying herself a doyenne of all she touched, she projected an accomplished air even as she lay dying. Everyone was amazed at the clarity of her mind right up to the end.

"Roses are still my favorite flower. You've brought me so many different ones." She reached over to the nightstand and turned off the radio that was playing the theme from *Shaft*.

The hospital was across town, a thirty-five minute drive; but I came for daily visiting estrangements. We regularly played the same game — chess, the one where everyone was her pawn. My moves were tolerance tempered with honesty, which often earned me banishment to the island of my mind—that coveted vacation spot for which we each have our own one-of-a-kind brochure.

Sitting next to her on the edge of her hospital bed, she gazed at me with clear eyes and a countenance that said *I have something important to tell you.* I leaned in a bit to allow for soft speaking—but not too far, since close body proximity, along with kissing and touching, was not a family tradition. Her matter-of-fact voice uttered her dying gift—"you really were a disappointment to me."

Oh...my...god, really?! That's it? Nothing else comes to mind! Wanna take a minute or two to confer with your conscience? What happened to the benevolence of the dying – one's legacy and all that? Damn, why aren't you dead yet? Doesn't matter, I have assurances that the morgue has a slab with your name on it. Thank god your organs can't be donated; no part of you should live on.

I couldn't move; and yet, I saw myself running out the door, down the hall, and into my car—careening for the sanctuary of home. I needed a shower to wash off the narcissism and retch her perspective spewed over my lifetime. My left leg ached as the cinder block edge of her bed started cutting into my thigh. All sounds stopped their overtures to instead stand at attention, except for the echo of her distinctive maternal devotion. The room shrank to the size of a thimble on a large thumb. I imagined the doctor writing an order to her two patrons:

Vulcan, for a proper pummeling, and Hades, for transport to apt accommodations.

Suffering is veiled opportunity echoed my therapist in my head. *Oh, there's what I need — fortune cookie wisdom.*

I turned the radio back on for distraction. The tune that popped up didn't register as I couldn't get Carly Simon out of my head — "You're So Vain," or was that "Leave Me Alone" by Helen Reddy; I don't recall.

Yeah, But... I Still Feel Bad About My Face

Lisa Solod

Some days I look in the mirror and I think: You look pretty good for a woman pushing 60. Other days I glance at myself and wonder: Who *is* that woman? She looks nothing like me. More than once I catch glimpses of my mother and my father in the way I look. And when I see photographs of my grandparents and parents when they were the age I am now I am both stunned and saddened. My parents look as I remember them, young and beautiful. My grandparents look like old people. Nice old people but old people nonetheless.

I am not sure what 59 is supposed to look like. That's the number on my next birthday, upcoming in a few weeks. What I do know is that I do not have the face I had at 19, 29, 39 or even 49. It has thinned, it has wrinkled, it has...elongated. It resembles my other faces but it isn't *quite* what I think it is when I don't look at it. I have been looking at my face for more than half a century and I should be used to the changes. But I'm not.

Recently I asked my son if I looked like the mother he had as a child. He took the question seriously (I like that about him) and said, thoughtfully: *I don't know. I would have to look at photographs. You are not unfamiliar*, he said.

I am not unfamiliar.

§

Part of the reason I feel bad about my face is that for too many years I did not accept that youth and heredity had been kind to me. I had no real idea. I know from memory and photographs that at 14 I changed quite dramatically: off came the braces and the glasses; I learned how to properly wear my hair; my body caught up to my boobs, and perhaps most importantly that small amount of confidence was just enough to propel me to expand my mind and my horizons rather than obsess about why I wasn't a cool blonde cheerleader/homecoming queen. I was no longer homely. But I wish I had been slightly more grateful. Perhaps I would feel less bad about my face now had I been more aware then.

When my boyfriend tells me I am beautiful, I tell him: You should have seen me years ago. Apparently I really *was* beautiful then. In fact, a friend just sent me a photo of myself from 20 years ago. I recognize that woman but, boy, does she look young. The face my boyfriend knows is the face he met at 54: to him I will remain that face forever (or at least I can hope). He can never know me prettier. Or younger. But he also won't know me far more insecure. This is, I suppose, not a bad thing.

It isn't fashionable to admit to feeling bad about how you look because if you do and if you do anything about it (like surgery or fillers) people will mercilessly attack you for feeling bad about your face AND for doing something about it. Unless, of course, you're Nora Ephron and you write your fear funny. And besides, I feel fine about my *neck* (although I do notice a recent crepeiness); it's my face that has me in a sometimes tizzy.

And yes, I know beauty and the loss of it is a first-world problem, a supposed woman's issue, nothing compared to the death of the environment or the end of the world or anything huge and really worrisome. I am supposed to be grateful I am aging at all and not sick. Or dead. I need a disclaimer just to write this essay.

But I still feel bad about my face.

§

I have spent enough money on lotions and potions and tools and creams and makeup and serums and miracle wrinkle cures to feed a thousand people. I am sure of it. It isn't as if I really believe the hype but I buy into it anyway; a good part of me is convinced that the relative smoothness of my skin is due to this or another cream, rather than genetics or luck. Or even delusion. It is entirely possible, *probable* even, that my looks don't change at all day to day;

what changes is only how I *react* to my face. If I'm busy and things are going well I feel pretty; if I am laid low by illness or something tough is going on then I might spend far too much time in self-examination. And no face, no matter how beautiful, can stand up to a 10X mirror and the critical eye of an unsettled beholder.

And as I have been trying to write about the losses my face has suffered I am keenly aware that there are lots of things I could do about those losses. The recent kerfuffle around a noted actress's new face notwithstanding, plastic surgery has been around a long time. I can easily remember Elizabeth Taylor in *Ash Wednesday*, her gorgeous face wrapped in white gauze and her eyes hidden by huge dark glasses. I was 17 and contemptuous of women who would go to such lengths. What did I know? I still had years and years of youth on my side.

But while I am not averse to injections of all sorts, or peels or whatever else one can do without surgery, I am against surgery for myself because I am terrified of anesthesia, more terrified of the short-term memory loss that accompanies it (and grows more prevalent with age) and the possibilities that something could go wrong than I am of the surgery itself. I am also against surgery for myself because surgery is permanent and if I wind up with a face that is not familiar, then what do I do? It is hard enough living with the "naturally" changing face I have without having to deal with one

made by a doctor who is trying to turn me into
something I thought I wanted but have no real
idea of. On the other hand, Jane Fonda looks
damned good and if she gave me the number of
her surgeon and held my hand throughout the
procedure I might reconsider.

§

My mother was a gorgeous woman with an
arresting mien, more stunning than beautiful.
Hard to look away from. Individually her
features were gravely imperfect. But she was a
looker. For the past ten years she has had little
knowledge of how she looks or how badly she
has aged, or how her face has collapsed in on
itself. Alzheimer's has taken over her mind and
stolen her beauty. For the first couple of years
she fought back: she wore lipstick and mascara,
dressed elegantly, carried herself like a queen.
But all that is gone. Now her hair is fixed
against her desire. Her nails are painted
shocking colors by a group of young volunteers
who come to her in assisted living. She is
dressed by aides. She is not familiar. She is not
at all familiar. On the other side, my aunt, my
mother's sister, jokes that her own worsening
macular degeneration has an upside: she can no
longer see how old *she* looks: the wrinkles
blurred, the age spots not visible in her
blindness. For that tiny thing she remains
grateful even if her loss of vision has rendered
her far more helpless. But she can still see her
own decline as it is mirrored in her sister's face.

I neither wish to lose my mind nor my sight. So I suppose that if I am lucky enough to keep both then I will have to continue to confront my face. And sometimes feel bad about it.

Aging is a bitch. There isn't a woman I know who doesn't suffer from some vanity, no matter how ignoble we think it is. We may not color our hair but we fix our nails and our face; we may not wear makeup but we color our hair. We may not care much about shopping or clothes but we plunk down good money for skin care. And all of us have that moment when we pass by a mirror or a window and see ourselves and we are not familiar. Not familiar at all.

Online Dating
in the Golden Years
Nancy Smiler Levinson

At seventy-five, I am not so old that I should accept living the rest of my years confined to a narrow world of widowhood. While I'm no Mrs. America, neither am I toothless, face-lifted, or *Rubenesque* (only sporting a muffin-top midsection which can be tamed by squeezing into a Spanx).

I can sit comfortably with a snowy-topped, slightly stooped date, over a tuna melt in a delicatessen booth and converse on numerous topics — politics, literature, art, theater... Medicare, trustworthy auto mechanics in town... as well as ask thoughtful questions, yet not ones requiring TMI (too-much-information) answers:

Would you be comfortable talking about your wife?

When and how did you recognize your interest in: civil engineering? teaching folk music? competitive Scrabble? exploring caves? collecting miniature ceramics? learning Pashtu?

decorating cakes? Do your Siberian Husky and angora cat get on with each other? How long do you leave your turkey in the oven?

So, a few months ago I steeled myself and bravely *put myself out there*. Without a playbook on septuagenarian dating, I did it. I went online. A dating site. A hoot, if you will.

Friends warned *caution*. Yes, I am of sound mind enough knowing never to give out my social, bank or credit card information to anyone. No money lending either. Not under any circumstance. Ever! No leaving my purse unattended, and no mention of my mother's maiden or first pet's name.

Admittedly, I felt uncomfortable at the thought of kissing a strange man. I began in the direction of expecting to simply meet an honorable, interesting, fun, humorous, in-fair-shape companion, or what is known in the golden years as an "activity partner." Oh, and preferably a widower who also had a happy marriage and knew the anguish of lost love, the life spun upside-down, and then the human need to live it forward.

One by one the wizards behind the site's curtain offered that I "find [my] magic" with Phunnyguy, SparkyD, Victor4107226, MensaMan, Naturelover, Caretodance, RUlonelytoo, Dragonslayer… the widowed and divorced men behind those user names, marketing themselves as sincere, sunny, big-hearted, love to laff, highly-educated or not…

and at varying ages. *Caution* was required here, too. Ages can be true or false; photos dated, careers enhanced.

Then, how to consider men who "wink" or "favor" me, when aged 35, 42, 51... a young saxophonist in Shreveport, Louisiana "willing to relocate"; a 49-year-old in Pittsburgh seeking a "slim, attractive, redhead between 37 and 80"? Joke? Desperately lonely? Perverse? Very perverse? OMG.

Shapes and sizes across the board fluctuated from "trim 'n athletic," to "a few extra pounds," with several additionally boasting "excellent health" (lest a woman fear caretaking at this stage in life), while a handful candidly revealed prostate surgery, hip replacement, or trying to quit smoking.

Interests? Bridge, fine dining, motor home travel, beach walking, golf, fly fishing, museums, movies (old and new), music (listening and playing), antique shopping, swap meets... and an occasional individual wishing that some woman would believe that he water-skiis, sails, climbs rocks, plays tennis, and works out five days a week. One said he'd forgive a woman if she is "not a rocket scientist as long as she is intelligent." Another put-it-out-there-elder admitted being "thirsty to love."

An 88-year-old man, having read on my profile that I am a writer, wasted not a moment of his ticking time, emailed that his deceased wife had been a poet and proposed that I "relocate" to his home where I would be provided a writing room of my own. (You know, like Virginia Woolf wanted.)

Another wrote that he still mourned his wife and desired merely a compassionate woman for nightly phone (not pillow) talk.

Yet another, a retiree with whom I spoke, seemed smart and politically liberal enough for me, posted his history as having been a public health professor, a thoracic surgeon, dean of a medical school, and founder of a women's clinic in Ethiopia. What! Not just red flags, but an entire parade full! After spending an inordinate amount of time piecing together his real name, Googling and making far-off phone calls, as anticipated, each and every contention indeed was a disconnect.

To be sure, *I broke the ice* first with a few women-seekers. A Parisian (born), photographed appropriately in beret, with dimpled, beguiling smile, and a come-hither look in his twinkling eyes, entitled his response to my query about corresponding:

"Life is a great Art, the supreme art is to live it." Then, "Thank you, Madame, for your kind comments and most specifically about your interest in the crown of my favorite books list. I wonder if I could find the glue that ties most of them together, the theme that unites. The only one seemingly outside the realm is 'The Little Prince.'"

He signed off by copying and sending two

Paul Eluard poems, "And a Smile" and "Good Justice."

Despite no mention of meeting Madame for café au lait, I printed the poems for myself because they are beautiful and touching, then sighed, *Au revoir, Monsieur, you arrogant bastard.* Another man, age 72, a retired executive, replied, "I can't wrap my head around dating an older woman." (That's the thanks I got for being age-honest).

I met Al for coffee in a public place, public being protectively important, along with a friend being apprised of the place and time. I'd searched him first, reassuring myself that as professed, he indeed had written and published several biographies, including one on a Supreme Court Justice. Not bad. But he was inches shorter than the short height he'd claimed, and despite my recognizing Mickey Rooney with multiple wives and Tina Fey inches taller than her husband, I couldn't find a mature-enough comfort zone to accept such a height difference for me.

While sipping cappuccino foam, Al dived right into relating his lifestyle — a first marriage ending in divorce, a second that became an open marriage until it exploded, and a third wife dying and leaving him a widower. Wait. There's more to this checkered scallywag. Since her passing he'd had three serious relationships but they, too, had dissolved.

True or not, I thought only OMG what stuff

goes on, what stories people have to tell, what lives human beings live!

After briefly sharing the short story of my long union, my husband's protracted illness, and my struggle caregiving, we talked a bit about history and biographies, however, he didn't appear particularly interested in the books I'd written for young adults (one each on Columbus and Magellan). Nor did he offer to buy a Starbucks croissant or cakepop for me to enjoy with my tall decaf cap.

A handshake departure and a *nice to meet you* clinched a strong mutual non-interest. Not a match.

I met MartinT for coffee. Was his online photo photoshopped? Now, don't rebuke me. I am not judgmental. I don't seek gorgeous or even good looking. This man simply was not appealing. He was unattractive from top to midriff (above the table line), revealing a saucer-sized stain on an ill-fitting houndstooth jacket. Hair was combed down over protruding ears.

At some point he complimented me, gee I'm a good listener, of course unaware that I could barely force myself to talk at all. Mostly, I nodded, a live bobblehead.

It's hurtful to label anyone a *loser*. The word itself disheartens me. Sadly, though, I realized that essentially he'd been rejected his entire life. On his profile he'd checked his status: divorced. I learned outright without a blink that he'd been in a marriage of thirty-some years, but his wife had never really loved him.

I felt like crying for MartinT, especially when he spoke of next time showing me some of his paintings rendered in a community art class.

With sincere pity for someone else, rather than my ongoing self-pity at missing my husband, I responded that I'm sure his paintings must be lovely, but I wasn't comfortable, not ready for a relationship, only relearning how to *date*. Crestfallen, he shuffled to the parking lot and drove off. I wept (inside) for the poor misbegotten thing.

Well, I'd put myself out there, and with hope fading, I decided to step up my adventure, maybe go a little wild, and I answered a message from Cowboyhank.

Pictured in a ten-gallon hat and with a horse. Posted: age 78, six-two, one-eighty pounds, blue eyes (it's a category, but does anyone care about eye color?), and lives on a ranch a couple hours from L.A.

This could be a true hoot! And what a kick it would be to crow about dating a dude!

Cautiously, not giving out my phone number or real email address, I called from my cell phone, so he'd not catch my home caller ID. He was living on his family-owned ranch, then up for sale. Meanwhile, he was involved creating a software program having something to do with agriculture, not a word of which I understood.

A week later he emailed through the online

connection that he was coming to the city on Saturday and why don't we meet for coffee mid-day. (Not Starbucks) With that arrangement confirmed we exchanged real names, which then gave me the gunshot to Google.

Wide-eyed at my computer screen, I gasped. There appeared a document, "Review Department of the State Bar Court. Public Matter Designated for Publication."

Cowboyhankpanky had been an attorney practicing law many years in the past. The document exposed the story of how he had been disbarred after misappropriating clients' funds. Many clients. Big funds. On another matter, he had even been incarcerated, although he didn't serve his full 180-day sentence.

Seemed that he long had a money-management problem and all these decades later was likely looking to manage mine. With my heart forgetting to beat, I said to myself, "Well, little lady, you surely did get yourself roped in." Regaining a pulse, I struck the keyboard with force. Coffee meet cancelled. Not comfortable. Not ready.

A friend wondered why I hadn't told him the truth, that he had been found out, that I had the goods on him, that he ought to be reported to the site. Ever cautious and prudent, I screamed Never! He could find and lasso me, then bludgeon me to death.

So—my nearly wild ride with a cowboy/dude/jailbird rode right off the dusty trail before the sun set.

At this moment, sitting alone in a museum café with a paper pad and pen (no, I don't have an iPad or laptop) I'm thinking that writing, or the art thereof, actually is my closest, my best companion.

Then I sigh. Is remaining online worth it? If I do, I'd have to meet my match soon. Time is ticking. Even as I write, I am aging.

But, then, I review my *brave* escapade so far, cringe and think: if only I could be introduced personally to a gentleman or meet one in the library or inadvertently bump shopping carts with one at Trader Joe's, I'd be rid of this sad, demoralizing quest. Meanwhile, I haven't shut down my membership yet. (You know what Emily Dickinson said about hope.)

What I'll Give You Since You Didn't Really Ask

Carol Graf Snyder

Introduction

Hey there kids—

Back when I was fired/laid off/retired
(roughly eight months after your father's
reinvention of himself which followed on the
heels of my mother's death and putting Rebel
down; I suspect you remember those days; I
regret not being mother-of-the-year at the time),
anyhow, back then, after my co-workers
extended their *so sorry, thank God it wasn't me*
sympathy, the boldest asked the mean little
question: *what next?* Of course I answered
collages. They'd seen the one I did for the
company's Holiday Decoration Contest 19??
(remember? but why would you? you were
busy with your own mold-growing bread or
volcano eruption projects; but I did win first
prize, I'd like to point out—a day off with pay;
N.B.: never took the day off… let that be a
lesson), so my colleagues accepted the lame
answer *collages.*

Once my future unemployment was assured, co-workers were more than happy to share their insights. After all, they were still employed, so they must have known something I didn't. Not wanting to look like a poor loser, I took much of their counsel in the spirit in which it was offered. But a few suggestions weren't half bad. The pearl of wisdom relevant to this journal: use your no-longer-working hours to get your life in order so you can slip out gracefully, allowing your children to take up where you left off without bumps or fuss. (Examples were provided but I won't take up your time, which would probably count as *fuss*).

Anyhow, as luck would have it, decades before I was beaten and robbed and left half dead by the side of the road, I'd stood in front of a gift shoppe's wall staring at rows of blank journals (My Spiritual Journey; It's a Dog's Life; Days in the Garden; My Travels; A Personal History; Our Wedding; Baby's First Year; My Prayer Journal… Fitness Journal… Personal Healthcare Journal; Birds I've Seen; Fish I've Caught; Horses I've Ridden; Liquor I've Drunk; Books I've Read… you get the idea).

I chose *My Possessions*, a slim leather volume in mauves and grays and what I can only call a Victorian font. In the years since, I'd thought of those pages lying blank as possessions crammed their way into my rooms, death after death after wrenching *how-did-it-all-slip-away-so-fast* death. Point: as is evident in the massive book one of you kids is holding, right now I can't put my fingers on the slim volume. Must be buried somewhere under strata of more recent acquisitions. But my possessions—a list of, I mean—wouldn't have fit in the faux-Victorian booklet anyhow.

So—here we go. A catalogue of everything that, taken together, should give you a picture of what your mother was. A catalogue of those things that might help you understand where you came from. And maybe where you're going?

Related Matter

A suggestion on the dispersal of items listed in this journal: start with the oldest child and work down. First you, Liz, pick the piece you'd most like. Then your turn, Ella. Next Bobby, then start over again and again and again… until (weeks later?) everything is gone. Whatever remains, call in the estate sale people and split the receipts.

So: God save my soul and give me fair skies as I make this journey.

Inventory

Sofa and Armchairs, Bedroom Dresser and Bedside Chests (All Colonial Williamsburg Furniture Reproductions made by Kittinger Company; historical site and quality furniture company—an interesting partnership; ended in 1990)

When your father and I were engaged long distance, we decorated the loft, each from his/her own city, thumbing through volumes that were more historical treatise than sales catalogue.

Reupholstered but in suitably good damask. Cabriole legs with gashes from Mrs. Daley's vacuum cleaner. (Who remembers: *Who cleaned the house today? Mrs. Daley. But she doesn't come daily, she comes weekly. But she's not weak, she's strong.*)

The stuff's not your style—but don't just drag it onto the sidewalk for the trash-night marauders to pick up (which, by the way, is a better end than having the unwanted ground up by the trash truck's packer blade). Put in a consignment shop. $$$$.

Or turn it into your style. Keep the expensive, good (but scratched) bones and do your own reupholstery; use some funky (??? is that still the word) fabric that shows you're on the right side of the joke.

Christmas Decorations

Seven 18-gallon, red Rubbermaid bins and five 31-gallon gray bins with big red stickers— full of Christmas, new. That is, nothing inherited. Somehow your Aunt Claire ended up with the ornaments from my childhood (spent entirely at 19 Wenzel St, Louisville, MA2-8880; I'm sure you haven't forgotten the house, so many happy hours visiting; but some day you may need the exact address to confirm that you're sitting outside looking into the window of the right partially gutted shot gun in

Butchertown).

Most binned decorations were purchased before your birth, back when your Dad and I were wandering in a snow globe world (one box contains a very old, heavy glass Austrian snow dome that your Dad and I picked up in a Viennese antique shop when we back-packed through *Europe on $5 a Day*; poor man, he trekked the rest of Europe with it on his back).

Maybe you should just divide up the holiday items by bin. Unwrapping ornament after ornament from tissue paper would take you into Easter (2 bins, labeled with big yellow stickers).

Curio filled with Lead Figures (Hollow cast cowboys and Indians, circus figures, zoo animals, skaters and sledders and city folks in '30s attire; workmen of all trades).

Before you children, there wasn't one city I visited on business trips without searching its antique/thrift/junk stores for these things. When we were engaged, your father shared memories of visiting Stewart's 4th floor toy section with his great aunts. Right before they lunched in the very proper dining room and boarded the train back home, they allowed him to select two lead favorites. He spent some of his happiest childhood hours on the floor, alone, playing with his collection. (See print *Solitary Boy Playing Out His Dreams* on the wall of the t.v. room).

Addendum: When your dad went off to college, his mother gave the entire collection to the St. Vincent de Paul thrift shop.

Hoosier Cabinet

Belonged to your great-grandmother (my mother's mother, Adela Rausch nee Zwick, born in Stegersbach, 1888; came to America when 16, worked in the house of a wealthy family, married my grandfather Gustav who'd immigrated from the Austrian farming town one over from hers, Olbendorf?).

Cabinet was in the breakfast room of what had been Grandma's home with Grandpop and Uncle Tobias all through my youth (119 Franklin St., SH4-1440).

Family friend/distant relative from Austria, Katie Vogl, spoke up for the cabinet when UT died and the house was being sold: *if no one was interested, always admired it, such fond memories of Adela standing there baking.* My Aunt Elena was *so sorry* (Mom would have been too reserved to speak up; fortunately not so her sister): *Maria Theresa asked for only that to remember her grandma by.* So here you have the thing, beaming in high gloss because Grandpop varnished it, along with all other 119 Franklin furniture to keep away dust and the accompanying agents of destruction.

Crumber (hammered aluminum marked Hand Wrought, Rodger Kent #444)

The Hammered Aluminum Collectors website notes that Rodger Kent is not the name of the engineer/designer but rather the names of the two intersecting streets seen from the engineer/designer's office window when trying to think up a name for the new giftware line he was designing. (Incidentally, the "not Rodger Kent" engineer/designer was almost fired from the company but survived those trying times to *show them* and become owner).

As a child at what seemed great dinners in Grandma's house (see Hoosier Cabinet entry), before dessert I'd stand in the doorway between breakfast room and adult dining room and watch Grandma whisk away the remains of the meal into the crumber with the matching brush. Seemed so genteel. Until decades later your father pointed out hammered aluminum was the poor man's silver popular in the depression through the '50s.

4" by 3" Metal Die Cut Pirate Skull and Cross Bones Chest (on dresser)

Given to me by my Uncle Tobias (Mother's youngest brother; the Rausch siblings in birth order since you didn't meet them all: my mom, Uncle Stefan, Aunt Elena, Uncle Tobias). I believe the chest was filled with gold-foiled chocolate coins. That would make sense since there is a slit in the top. Of course it is a bank — I remember the clink, clank of metal against metal when I returned home from Grandma and Grandpop's with the two dimes Grandpop would slip into each of our hands. *Pop, you don't have to do that* — but he did. Each visit.

Contents of Pirate Chest

Jewelry given to me by my grandma's neighbors who must have been cleaning out their drawers. Thrifty sorts, survivors of the depression. They couldn't toss anything, even paste and glass and base metal painted gold. Though the stuff isn't without charm. Says something about those long gone folks.

Note, however, the prim bracelet of linked flat flowers with rose tourmaline centers. Of higher quality — gold filled; use one of the magnifying glasses in my collection to see the jeweler's mark; my eyesight is too bad to figure out anything but *gold filled*. There are sites for identifying the hundreds of vintage marks. Anyhow, I thought the thing was so special that I once wore it to school, grade 4 or 5? Sr. Felicita or Sister Mary Cecilia? What was I thinking? I spent the day kneeling in the corner, thinking of the tears the BVM wept because of my vanity. (Jimmie Ray and the other bad boys *boo-hoo'd* at me the rest of the week.)

Breakfront

The monstrosity from Wenzel Street that forces diners at the north end of my table to pull in their chair so tight that they are probably uncomfortable during the meal. I never sit there.

French Provincial style.

Mom's alcoholic, loud-mouthed, vaguely hare-lipped brother (Uncle Stefan) had once told his fun-loving wife (Debbie Sue; from Sweet Pea Mobile Home Park, was off 44, gone now): *Look at Annika. She buys one good dress to your every five cheap ones and she always looks classy.* Mom took this as a compliment.

So Mom and Dad waited until we kids were gone, then went to… ??? (Wish I could remember the furniture store's name, out in one of those suburbs where every Butchertown family hoped to end up.)

Anyhow, *French Provincial* — always the Wenzel Street aspired-to style, right through two sets of immigrant mahogany castoffs.

Linens

In breakfront drawers: doilies and pillowslips embroidered in backstitch, cross-stitch, French knots, eyelet, running, strait, seed or satin stitches (the stitching I can name). Appliqued runners. Ecru tatted butterflies, angels, snowflakes. Crocheted antimacassars (a word as ugly as the item; protected chair back and arms from grubby visitors leaving their oils on plush upholstered sofas; always hated them, but they are my past and your past is something you can't deny).

Each piece done by either my mother or grandmother. Each wrapped carefully in tissue, regrettably unlabeled. Impossible to tell which was made by whom.

(You'll see pawed-through piles of such handiwork on beds at estate sales. Almost as sad as the boxes of bent, discarded black and white photographs.)

Additional Breakfront Contents

Good China, twelve place settings and additional serving pieces (Theodore Haviland Limoges France, Small Roses in Yellow & Turquoise, around 1900)

Handed down from your father's great uncle—used for formal Washington dinners. Don't know his name (Wilson's war secretary 1913-16; sounds as if he was shown the door during Wilson's second term). I could look his name up but just ask your father. Good heavens, what am I thinking? Must have been Garrison. Of course it would have been your father's *paternal* grandfather's brother. Twelve double-handled soup tureens wouldn't have been number enough for feeding the junkyard dogs on your dad's *maternal* side of the family. (May I be a kinder mother-in-law so I won't be written about in a snarky junior high-ish hand—if any of you ever get married.)

Not sure why your father left the fine china here, despite his love of throwing great parties in fabulous style. Though a hundred plus pieces of fragile china would have been a damned nuisance for him to move. And an even more damned nuisance to wrap and pack in front of his sad-eyed children.

Sterling Flatware Set for 12 (Schofield Baltimore Rose pattern around 1900)

Like the china, I'm surprised it's still here in the breakfront.

Truth be told: after each of your father's visits to see you kids, I'd count the silver. I'd make a full reconnaissance of the house. Check bookcases for missing volumes: your father's father's leather Shakespeare volumes. His *Canterbury Tales*.

Fuller truth be told: while he visited, I went through his Milano leather duffel bag, unfolding papers, flipping through his matching travel phone book, looking through those many interior pockets and hidden compartments found in men's luxury travel cases.

I once had a dream that, after dropping your dad off at the train station, I returned home to find paintings and the Davenport-listed prints gone, with empty, rectangular shapes covering the walls. His great aunt's jewelry missing from my jewelry box. (Jewelry box: the vintage wooden multi-drawered toolbox my dad had bought, used, for his smaller, more exacting tools. N.B.: all fine jewelry in the upper drawers is from your father's side. Only the bottom drawer holds stuff my siblings and I bought for Mom for Christmas and birthdays. At Kresge's—after the *how lovely*'s, did she ever wear any of it? I seem to remember the outrageous green and pink protuberances around her neck once when making our weekly bus trip to Grandma and Grandpop's. All I can really prove is that each piece we gave her was wrapped in tissue. Even though synthetic not semi-precious, don't pitch. There are hoards of '50s costume jewelry collectors who'll give you a few dollars… but I digress. God keep me on course in this churning sea.)

Anyhow, I awakened from the dream about the house being stripped — recurrent nightmare, actually — to find the place always intact. Everything where your father had left it when he moved on with his life.

I suppose some would say that is evidence of your father's being, underneath it all, a good man. One who doesn't snap a bruised reed or snuff out the smoldering wick. One who recognizes his responsibilities despite ensuring his *right to be happy*. I'd tell those "some" — bullshit. Right after I snapped their reed and snuffed their smoldering wick.

As the nuns said, *life is a vale of tears*. And as we hike through it, our job is to meet our *responsibilities*, not fret over our *rights*.

Small Steamer Trunk (Used by my father when he left his mother, siblings and homeland and crossed the Atlantic. You'll open it thinking it contains his youth, but it never did. In fact, the only things I remember Mom saying he brought and kept as memento were three brand-new handkerchiefs from his mother. Hand sewn? Surely. Wonder what happened to them?)

Trunk contains love letters:

1) To me, away at college, from Mom. With a dear one sentence comment at the end written by my dad. Mom was the business school graduate so all such matters were hers. But theirs was what I guess we'd now call a *loving partnership,* and Dad cherished his family — so he always left his mark.

2) My college letters to my long-since dead brother. (His lock of hair is in the envelope labeled by undertaker *Eddie's Lock of Hair* in bottom jewelry box drawer — a Victorian death memento of sorts. If I use the hair and/or labeled envelope in a future collage, I'll cross through these comments.)

Also the last Norcross greeting card I sent him:

> *Hi Eddie,*
>
> *Be sure to collect shopping bags full of Halloween grit for me. If Sidney is too slow, leave him behind. I'll be in late Halloween night – long after you are asleep – so please leave the loot on the kitchen table. Then I can start munching without waking you up.*
>
> *Love,*
>
> *Maria Theresa*

And my brother's last kitchen table note to me when I left after that Halloween visit:

> *Bye, Maria Theresa. Take whatever candy you want. Had fun playing checkers.*
>
> *I'll practice with Sidney – and beat you at Thanksgiving. Love, Eddie*

3) A love letter from your paternal grandfather to your unpleasant paternal grandmother (no comment needed; you won't forget that woman even if you eventually wander with me through the fields of dementia). Jammed into an envelope with her

sprawling, untutored handwriting saying: *This will explain it all*. (It didn't — but you can read; perhaps you're more sympathetic than I; she is your family, I suppose.)

4) Your father's letters to me. I can't look at them. They're for you to read — or not.

Actually, after writing the above, I took a break, had some baba ganoush from the farmer's market and read two of the letters with the earliest postmarks.

The first seems so hopeful:

> *I can think of nothing to add to this letter except that I love you. But then I guess there is really nothing else to say anyway and perhaps everything else is just trying to say that.*

The second, cautious:

> *On days like this I worry much about us. I want things to work out so desperately I cannot evade the fear that they might not. We have come far, we two together. That needs remembering.*

So genuine? With no plans of betrayal; no foreboding of what he would become — or rather, what he was but couldn't recognize.

Maybe his letters can be put to good use. However, if you don't find them in the trunk and I haven't used them in one of the unsold collages that you're probably tripping over as you try to clean out the house, then I've destroyed them. (Can I start a fire in the unused fireplace? That was always your father's job, starting fires. Amusing — I see another collage taking shape.)

Perhaps your father's letters are too depressing a legacy to pass on — proving as they may that even the best of folk can't love purely. Love is not eternal (despite much literature to the contrary, such as that Rupert Brooke poem "The Call" — I'll create an appendix for it; not half-bad). Love's a token to put into the fare box so you can be shuttled somewhere else. (In the pirate's chest you'll find two tokens with a stencil cut *T* in the center, an incised *L* on the left, *C* to the right, for Louisville Transit Company — long since renamed TARC; tokens used to get me to/from high school.)

I may tear this page out.

§

Awakened this morning in a dream of fire and bullets, the sea blazing to darkness, the black body in its shroud, dog-tags welded to breastbone.

That sounded pompous — and isn't quite true. I actually thought of "Burning the Letters" at coffee this morning. I looked for my Randall Jarrell — God knows, could be in any of the unseen back rows in the basement bookcases. But found a copy on line. (I'll add it to the section with the Brooke so you don't have to search the web; always irritating.)

We take what we want from things, bits and pieces of the whole and leave other bits and pieces lying there, outside our line-of-vision, eventually forgotten. So I took out all the Christ allusions from the Jarrell and left just the facts: a pilot's wife burned her dead husband's letters. Never believed it, never will, but just maybe she was wealthy or powerful or wise or broken enough to know something I can't.

And thinking along those two-penny lines, I realize what your father accomplished in taking off with an empty suitcase after deciding to (not-literally) burn his "letters." He left the burden of the past to me. And I, not as brave as your duplicitous father, clutched at it, the buoyant coffin that gets us to shore when the triumphant voyagers sink into new seas.

And here I was, about to foist all this on you three.

So: what I'll give you since you really didn't ask: just the William Carlos Williams red wheelbarrow thing—no oppressive memories, no nagging expectations, no ties to bind (though I do have to mention there's a small wheelbarrow in the garage, the appropriate city-size for the mean little plot that was my father's in his new country). Simply the moment after the rain stops and the wide-eyed sky listens to the hush before breaking open with light. Just a house full of stuff that, if you don't find it beautiful or useful, pitch—without fear of me turning in my grave.

Take Me Home
Alan D. Harris

Friday
June 10, 1983

For the last two days I couldn't get that image out of my head. To see Grandpa's pants down around his knees on the bathroom floor still haunted me. On my way home from school I walked past his house. And not unlike his glass eye, the headlights on the old Lumina looked right through me. The porch light was still on, waiting for Grandpa's return.

As soon as I got home I threw my backpack on the kitchen table. Today's newspaper was lying there opened to Dad's favorite section — the obituaries. I purposely set my backpack over the list of names and photos of people who smiled for the camera not knowing what page of the paper their smile would end up in. I pulled out the sports section and walked over to the fridge. In the freezer was a Kit Kat. Mom knows how I love my chocolate like Grandpa loves his beer — cold. Dad was up pretty late at the hospital; both he and Mom still went to work today as usual. The house was quiet. I had only the sports section to share my Kit Kat with. I tried to read but all I could think about was Grandpa's boxers down around his knees like he'd been pantsed in gym class and kicked to the ground by the schoolyard bully. I was hoping the taste of chocolate would help me forget.

Maybe chocolate helps you remember because I learned that it sure doesn't help you forget.

The phone rang at 3:19 in the afternoon. I was afraid to answer. I was afraid it was the hospital—the Sisters of Mercy. I was afraid one of the sisters had to tell someone that Grandpa was dead. I didn't want to be that someone. As long as the call didn't come, as long as no one answered the phone, he was still alive. I watched it ring several times, wishing it could tell me who was calling. I remember Grandpa telling me once to be careful what you wish for, because one day it'll come true.

Because there was no sense waiting for someday, I took another bite of a cold Kit Kat and answered the phone. The caller heard me mumble a scared "Hello?"

The voice on the other end said, "Don't talk with your mouth full, Soldier."

"Grandpa!"

"The Sisters without Mercy are charging me extra to use their rotary-dial phone. This place is like the sixties without any hippies. So let's make it quick," he said. "Tell me—what happened?"

"Your pants were down around your knees."

"And... ?"

I called that new emergency phone number on your rotary dial phone. It works, the ambulance was pretty quick."

"What new emergency phone number?"

"9-1-1."

"9-1-1-what?"

"That's it, just 9-1-1. I guess it gives you a chance to get ready for the ambulance."

"Tell me you pulled up my pants."

"Nope."

"What happened next?"

"I let the ambulance people in — two of them, a man and a woman. Both in uniforms and wearing plastic gloves. The woman was the first one in the bathroom."

"Oh, boy."

"She shouted to the other, *Elvis down!*"

"Everybody loves the King."

"Who?"

"Is that it? There's got to be more. Who brought my Navy cap?"

"The old hat that says USN?"

"There's flowers here too, like someone robbed a funeral home."

"You were asleep yesterday. I heard you're hypo-something something."

"Short on sugar."

"So Dad sat with you all day and most of the night. He brought that stuff."

"Your father probably went through my pockets. What else happened?"

"The Red Wings didn't get Pat Lafontaine. They got some skinny kid named Yzerman."

"Really?"

"Really." There was a long silence. The only sound I could hear was the sound I made each time I took a breath. I was afraid until finally he let me know that he was still alive.

"If that's the worst thing that happened—I can live with it. Tell the old man..."

"You're the only old man I know."

"Listen, Soldier. I need you to tell your father something important."

"Cool—you guys are finally talking. What do you want to say to him?"

"Bring me home," he said as the phone clicked and once more the sound of my own breathing was all that remained.

Everything is Doggy

Wolfgang Niesielski

Another birthday is coming up quickly for me, although I could have sworn I had just celebrated this exact event a mere couple of months ago. Now, for a very young person a year might be the equivalent of a decade for a more senior one. Why? Mostly, I think, because of repetition — been there, done that. Life becomes a boring array of sameness and monotony, nothing new and exciting to write home about, as time zips by. But I'm determined this "zipping by" business has to change!

Let's say you're a three-year old (yes, you once were a toddler, even though you don't remember much). Most likely you'll block out all the eventful adventures of never-ending diaper-filled days, the endless sucking of thumbs and eternal throwing of tantrums that resulted from your assumption that your caretaker, who had merely stepped out of your line of vision, had abandoned you. One year for you then was exactly one third of your life — a very long time.

From the standpoint of an adult though it

might not be all that exhilarating and thrilling because not a lot would have happened. So far vast portions of your life would have been consumed with endeavors like attempting to walk upright without immediately toppling over. Intellectual pursuits would have been largely focused on the mysterious contents in your belly button. And conversations and exchange of ideas with family and friends would also have been extremely limited, mostly because your entire vocabulary would have consisted of branding any and all furry creatures on four legs with the label "doggy." That's not much to put on your résumé, is it? No wonder toddlers rarely get hired.

Now, let's look at a ninety-year-old. Although such a person might have problems with employment as well, and his days, as I understand, might be filled with some of the abovementioned activities also, he can however boast that one-third of his or her life comprises a whole of thirty years, not just one. That's nothing to sneeze at. While, for a small infant, one single day may hold the promise of never-ending thrilling new adventures and excitement, for a ninety-year-old, one day is just a blip on the radar screen!

So from now on, I'm taking a lesson from three-year-olds. I'll look at things afresh, as if I experience them for the first time. Live in the moment will be my motto. That should go a long way in slowing things down. This may actually cause me to wonder about the profusion of candles on my birthday cake. What a misuse of good wax, three would have been plenty. The only problem I see, experiencing things brand-new, is with the consumption of beer at my birthday party. Beer is an acquired taste and it took me a long time building up a tolerance for it. I hate to have all that work go to waste now. Also, I wouldn't want to have my wife arrested for contributing to the delinquency of a minor—the new me. So, I may have to allow for a few adjustments, which might also include tolerating snide remarks by my playmates about a certain number, an inflated figure that will quite tastelessly be displayed on inflated balloons all over the place.

But my new philosophy would really come in handy while opening those birthday packages. I naturally would be taken aback about the clever design of a bottle opener, shaped like the torso of a woman, for example. And it would take me hours to comprehend the meaning of the words on my new flashy tie, "Over the hill, but still kickin'." But what use could I possibly have for supposedly hilarious birthday cards proclaiming the virtues of canes, walkers and adult diapers?

Eventually, though, to prove my real age I will stomp my foot and throw a tantrum, complaining tearfully that I actually had wished for a pony.

Willing Branches
J. L. Cooper

I was seven when it first occurred to me I was growing older like everyone else. I was looking down from an airplane window, scanning the Grand Canyon for its layered secrets. I felt miniscule, and or course I was, but it didn't frighten me so much as wake me. I looked at my hands and they were still mine. I touched the airplane window, as if to anchor myself to the difference between near and far.

In teen years, I was always in motion, running between points A and B. I would light fuses on fireworks before I knew much about their dangers. I even made some new variations of pinwheels. The important part is to find the center and nail it in a piece of solid wood, so when it spins, it won't wobble out of control. The sensible side of me made practical inventions, and I collected beautiful coins. My favorites were the walking liberty half-dollar and the seated liberty dime. I never understood the plainness of coins that were minted later.

In my twenties, I jumped from one boxcar to another on a moving train through the Nevada desert under a full moon. I fell in love with randomness, and tried to give it meaning. Jazz clubs called me in the late hours. I found I had kindness in me, and opened to a fondness for unlikely people. I could not have made them up in the turbulence. I had fear, and plenty of confusion. My efforts to love were a brew of mixed desires. So sweet, the discoveries — so painful, a few. I made enduring friends, but wasn't prepared for the abyss of loss until I was in it.

I asked what stream I wanted to swim, and began to study intensely. I studied as if lesser ideas were profound, then left books for a camera and a trumpet, but came to see I didn't have to exclude anything just because my muse moved on. When I returned to books, I had a more critical mind but also a touch of sad awareness. Knowledge felt relative, skewed by the wanting.

In my thirties I was superman, loving my wife and children. My career as a psychologist moved faster than the river. Every summer, I'd hold my breath a minute or more, gliding underwater in the current of the American River, six inches above the rocks and clay. I'd come up for air, then go down again. The river ran parallel, I suppose, to other rivers in my mind.

I couldn't stop replaying a soliloquy from a man I saw ranting in a market in Aberdeen, Scotland. "Wake up," he kept shouting. There I was, the only person who stopped to listen to him suffer on the busy street. He was lamenting the waste of life, but there he was, alone and angry. What kind of paradox made me stop to listen? I thought I was already awake. There was also a grizzled fisherman I met in the Shetland Islands, who said he knew me when it couldn't possibly have been true. "Don't waste your life on land," he advised. Then he kept on drinking. I see his face in every gale.

The next two decades were the deepening kind. I was chased by a somber ghost, and had tantalizing visions of clarity. I found mysteries in the two-way street of time. My children grew up and went on their own adventures, while my wife and I took cha-cha lessons. My work led to levels I wouldn't have guessed as a younger man. I found myself looking at my hands more often, and saw the little lines around our eyes that were never there before. She had the same smile as always. The place where my dog used to sit, by the large window in the living room, still draws my eyes in the morning. I can easily see her in my mind and summon the silk of her coat. Something wonderful about a tall, not too bright, English Setter. She used to stare out the window like a statue, noticing every passing car and person as if everything in the universe was new.

I suppose I'm like the canyon now, layered and dense, maybe too serious, cut by rivers and winds, leaning toward a kiss of lemonade, dancing salsa in the kitchen with my wife, on the cusp of sixty-five. The orange blossoms are in full bloom. When they're gone, the lemon blossoms come. The gardenias will have a second go, then the jasmine. There's a waxing crescent moon, but I'm back among the orange blossoms, eyes closed. I see white spiral heavens, little galaxies whose fragrance took millions of years to reach the moment of a single inward breath. The willing branches seem to know me. They grow when I'm not paying attention. Look, I'm seven again. What kind of magic is this?

Author Bios

Bruce Alford's first collection, *Terminal Switching* was published in 2007 (Elk River Review Press). He received a Master of Fine Arts from the University of Alabama and was an assistant professor of creative writing at the University of South Alabama from 2007-2011. Before working in academia, he was an inner-city missionary and journalist. He has published fiction, creative nonfiction and poetry in journals such as the *African American Review, Comstock Review, Imagination & Place Press, Louisiana Literature*, and many others. He currently lives in Hammond, Louisiana.

Barry Antokoletz was honored to have another story, 'A Facts-of-Life Primer,' published in The Connecticut Review, Fall 2012 edition. He also has several short stories dealing with relationships, and a sci-fi novel near completion eager to see the public light. Born in 1946 and raised in the Bronx, Barry earned his English Literature degrees at CCNY and SUNY-Stony Brook. Over the ensuing decades, he taught English composition and literature at CUNY and Western Connecticut State University, as well as ESL in Vienna and Hiroshima. He currently lives with his two children in Brewster, New York, and can be contacted at jcln99@yahoo.com.

Judith Arcana (72) writes poems, stories, essays—and books, including *Grace Paley's Life Stories, A Literary Biography* and the poetry collection *What if your mother.* Judith's story, *Soon To Be A Major Motion Picture*, won the first Minerva Rising Prose Prize, and came out as a chapbook in 2015. Also recent are a set of three lyric broadsides, *The Water Portfolio* (2014); a fiction zine, *Keesha and Joanie and JANE* (2013); and a poetry chapbook, *The Parachute Jump Effect* (2012). 'The Woman Who Hands You A Gun' was first published in *Cirque* (Winter Solstice/2012). Visit www.juditharcana.com.

Anthony Bain studied at the London School of Journalism, then has spent the last 12 years living in Barcelona and sharing his writing about the city for *The Barcelona Metropolitan*. He has also published short stories for *Paper Tape* magazine and the *Lowestoft Chronicle*.

Susanne Braham (70) has recently retired from editing for Columbia University after more than 17 years. She began writing in earnest after her 56-year-old husband's sudden death in November 2002. Several of her poems were published in two anthologies about widowhood, a few humorous pieces have been published online, and she can't remember at the moment where the rest of her writing has gone—but it's out there somewhere. Contact her at sb559@columbia.edu or 2 East End Avenue (5F), New York, NY 10075-1153; 212-744-1688.

Kevin Carey (58) teaches in the English Department at Salem State University. He has published two books—a chapbook of fiction *The Beach People*, from Red Bird Chapbooks (2014) and a book of poetry *The One Fifteen to Penn Station*, from Cavankerry Press, N.J. (2012). He has also co-directed and produced a documentary film about New Jersey poet Maria Mazziotti Gillan, called *All That Lies Between Us*. A new collection of poems, *Jesus Was a Homeboy*, (CavanKerry Press) is due out in the fall of 2016. More info at Kevincareywriter.com.

Adrian Ernesto Cepeda (44) is an LA poet who's currently enrolled in the MFA Graduate program at Antioch University in Los Angeles where he lives with his lovely wife and their adorably spoiled cat Woody

Gold. His poetry has been featured in forty different publications including *The Yellow Chair Review, Edgar Allen Poet Journal #2, Sling Magazine, Thick With Conviction, Luna Luna Magazine* and *Silver Birch Press*.

J. L. Cooper is a clinical psychologist and writer in Sacramento, California. His work explores the lyrical voice and the pursuit of imagery in the telling of a life. He is winner of First Place in *Short Short Fiction in New Millennium Writings*, 2013, and Second Place in *Essay in Literal Latte*, 2014. His work has appeared or is forthcoming in *Oberon, The Manhattan Review, Gold Man Review, Subliminal Interiors, Flutter Poetry Journal, The Sun (Reader's Write), Kind of a Hurricane Press*, and *Barrier Islands Review*. Email him at coopphd@earthlink.net.

Douglas K. Currier's (60) work appears in the anthology *Onion River: Six Vermont Poets*. Daniel Lusk, ed. Winooski, VT. Book Rack, 1997. He lives in Burlington, Vermont.

Born in Virginia, **Bill Cushing** (63) grew up in New York, attended school in Pennsylvania, began college in Missouri but quickly found himself back in Virginia and New York as well as Florida, Maryland, Texas, the Virgin Islands, and Puerto Rico before moving to California in 1996. Earning an MFA in writing from Goddard College in Vermont, Bill has had reviews, articles, and poems published in *Another Chicago Magazine, Birders World, Brownstone Review,* the *Florida Times Union, genius & madness, Metaphor, Sabal Palm Review,* the *San Juan Star,* and *Synergy*. He now teaches English at East Los Angeles and Mt. San Antonio colleges while 'growing old' with his wife Ghisela and their son Gabriel. He can be contacted at piscespoet@yahoo.com.

Diana Decker (62) has written poetry for decades, but only recently has let it see the light of day. Her work has appeared or is forthcoming in *Silver Birch Press, Poppy Road Review, Verdad Journal of Literature and*

Art, and *Mothers Always Write*. Diana writes, sings, and counts the birds on the small farm in Western New York that she shares with her husband. Follow her on Twitter at @diana_decker.

Liz Dolan's (74) poetry manuscript, *A Secret of Long Life*, nominated for the Robert McGovern Prize, Ashville University, and a Pushcart, has been published by Cave Moon Press. Her first poetry collection, *They Abide*, was published by March Street. An eight-time Pushcart nominee and winner of Best of the Web, she was a finalist for Best of the Net 2014. She won The Nassau Prize for Nonfiction, 2011 and the same prize for fiction, 2015. She has received fellowships from the Delaware Division of the Arts, The Atlantic Center for the Arts and Martha's Vineyard. Liz serves on the poetry board of *Philadelphia Stories*. She is most grateful for her ten grandchildren who pepper her life and who live on the next block.

Falconhead has appeared in *Night Train Magazine, The Rock River Review, Still Point Arts, Antiphon, FictionWeek Literary Review, The Red Line, The Corner Club Press, Naugatuck River Review, Outside In Literary & Travel Magazine, Wilde Magazine, Poetry Potion, Foliate Oak Literary Magazine, Thick Jam, Meat for Tea, Poetica Magazine, Camas: The Nature of The West, Thin Air Magazine, Huesoloco Journal, Glitterwolf, Whistling Fire, Two Hawks Quarterly, Rock & Sling, Adanna Literary Journal, Deltona Howl*, and Green Wind Press's *Words Fly Away* Anthology, among others, and is forthcoming in several more publications. For his poem 'Man-Made God *or* Poem In Which The Hypochondriac Gets His Way' *Emerge Literary Journal* awarded him 'runner-up' in their 2014 poetry contest. You can follow Falconhead on Twitter @Falconheadpens.

Adam Fisher's poems have appeared in a wide variety of publications including *LI Quarterly, LI Sounds, Manhattan Poetry Review, North Atlantic Review,*

Oberon, West Hills Review and *The NY Times*. His three books of poems are *Rooms, Airy Rooms* (published by Writers Ink Press and Cross Cultural Communications in cooperation with Behrman House), *Dancing Alone* (published by Birnham Wood/Long Island Quarterly), and *Enough To Stop The Heart* (published by Writers Ink Press). He won First Prize for Poetry at the 1990 Westhampton Writers Festival and one of the 1991 Anna D. Rosenberg poetry awards sponsored by the Magnus Museum in Berkeley. He was awarded a prize at the Mid-Island Y 2006 Adult Poetry Contest. In 2008 and 2009 he won a first prize in the Performance Poets Association contest. From 2006 to 2014 he was Poetry Editor of the CCAR (Central Conference of American Rabbis) Journal.

Alan D. Harris is a 60 year-old graduate student who writes short stories, plays, and poetry based primarily upon the life-stories of friends, family and total strangers. Harris is the 2011 recipient of the Stephen H. Tudor Scholarship in Creative Writing, the 2014 John Clare Poetry Prize, and the 2015 Tompkins Poetry Award from Wayne State University. In addition he is the father of seven, grandfather of seven, as well as a Pushcart Prize nominee in both 2013 and 2014. Mr. Harris now resides in East Lansing, Michigan.

Art Heifetz teaches ESL to refugees in Richmond Va. He started writing poetry to win the heart of a beautiful Nicaraguan. He is currently growing old. Rapidly. See polishedbrasspoems.com for more of his work.

Sarah Henry is a retired newspaper employee in the Pittsburgh area. Her poems have appeared locally in *The Pittsburgh Post Gazette, The Loyalhanna Review*, and *Poetry Explosion Newsletter*. Her poetry has also been published farther afield in *The Hollins Critic* and *Pegasus*, as well as other journals. Humor is very important to her. Email her at shenry6256@gmail.com.

Lynn Hoffman was born in Brooklyn and lives in Philadelphia. Among his published books are *Radiation Days*—a comedy about cancer and *Short Course in Beer*, a very serious but tasty book about ales and lagers.

Ann Howells's poetry appears in *Borderlands, Concho River Review, Crannog* (Ire*), RiverSedge, Rockhurst Review, San Pedro River Review* and *Spillway* among others. She serves on the board of Dallas Poets Community, 501-c-3 non-profit, and has edited *Illya's Honey Literary Journal,* since 1999, recently taking it digital (www.IllyasHoney. com) and taking on a co-editor with whom she alternates issues. Her chapbooks are, *Black Crow in Flight* (Main Street Rag Publishing, 2007) and *the Rosebud Diaries* (Willet Press, 2012). She has been read on NPR, interviewed on *Writers Around Annapolis* television, and been four times nominated for a Pushcart, twice in 2014.

Dustin Hyman started as a freelance writer and then became a journalist, but neither occupation gave him sufficient creative control. He teaches at the University of Louisiana, where he is working toward a PhD in English. His fiction has appeared in various places and his first novel, *Island Folks*, was published in 2014 by Black Rose Writing. Contact Dustin by email at dustinhyman@louisiana.edu.

Jennifer Lagier (66) has published nine books of poetry and has had poetry published in a variety of literary magazines. Her latest book, *Camille Vérité*, was just published by FutureCycle Press and is available on Amazon.com. She taught with California Poets in the Schools and is now a retired college librarian/ instructor, member of the Italian American Writers Association, co-edits the *Homestead Review,* maintains websites for *Homestead Review, Monterey Poetry Review, Ping Pong Literary Journal* and *misfitmagazine.com.* She also helps coordinate monthly Monterey Bay Poetry Consortium Second

Sunday readings. Visit her website at jlagier.net.

Nancy Smiler Levinson (75) is author of *Moments Of Dawn: A Poetic Memoir of Love & Family; Affliction & Affirmation*. Her prose poetry and stories have appeared in numerous journals including *Poetica, Touch, Blood and Thunder, Confrontation* and *Phantasmagoria*. She began her career in journalism, then turned to writing books for young readers, many of which won distinguished awards. The CNF here first appeared in Foliate Oak Literary Magazine, April 2015.

Amanda Lewan is a writer and editor. Her work has been featured in *The Nation, Niche Magazine, Journal of Americana* and more. You can follow her work at www.amandalewan.com.

Carol D. Marsh graduated in 2014, at age fifty-nine, from Goucher College's MFA in Creative Nonfiction program. Excerpts from her thesis—a memoir about living and working with homeless women with AIDS—have been published in *Soundings Review* (Honorable Mention, 2014 First Publication Contest), *Jenny Magazine*, and *bioStories* (March 2015 Featured Essay). Visit her website at www.caroldmarsh.com.

Sandy McPheron (63) has been a memoirist and essayist for many years. She has had her work included in several anthologies, won first place in *Tiny Lights Literary Journal* Essay Contest and was chosen to do a public presentation of her work at Speakeasy in Laurel Canyon, California. She lives with her husband of countless decades, and her rescue mutt in the foothills of Southern California. Sandy can be reached at smcpheron@mac.com.

Ed Meek's third book of poetry, *Spy Pond*, just came out with Prolific Press. His work has appeared in *The Paris Review, The North American Review, The Sun, The Boston Globe*, and other journals. He blogs at letsrethink.org, and his Twitter handle is @emeek.

Siena Milia is an avid world traveler and dedicated mother of four young children. She writes poetry and short stories, many of which have been published in online journals. Currently Siena is working on a literary novel set amid Iran's 1979 Islamic revolution and its aftermath. Siena lives with her husband and children in Saudi Arabia. Follow her work on twitter @sienamilia, on her blog sienamilia.tumblr.com, and at Describli.com.

Carol Murphy, MA, is a writer, consultant and speech-language pathologist who has written essays, interviews, stories and poems about children, language development, learning disabilities, the therapeutic and almost mystical influence of animals, and the many ways language, or a lack of it, colors life's experiences. Two of her stories were 'Likely Story', published by *Special Education Advisor* (www.specialeducationadvisor.com), and 'Auricle' published in *Good Dogs Doing Good*. She has also published professional articles and a newsletter for over twenty years. A few recently published stories are 'Becoming a Grandmother,' by an area news magazine, 'Whiffs' by Reddashboard Press, and 'Dispersion' by Solarwyrm Press. She finds daily inspiration for writing through her experiences with the interplay of communication and the many ways lives can go awry, or be set straight, simply by a precise word at a pivotal moment. She lives with her husband, two cats and a horse in Santa Cruz, CA. Writing has been a lifelong passion. A favorite quote is 'The limits of my language means the limits of my world.' (Ludwig Wittgenstein) She can be reached through her website at www.carolmurphy.org.

Wolfgang Niesielski was born in Germany, got a German first name and a Polish last name, due to the fact that his dad was born close to the Polish border and whose ancestors mixed with the folks next door (they seemed to have been very friendly people). He arrived in New York at the age of 22, hitchhiked across the states to California, where he finally got stuck observing the hippie culture of making love, instead of war, an experience necessitated a closer familiarizing of the various ins and out. He makes his living as an illustrator and cartoonist and writes a weekly humor column for *The Contra Costa Times* and other publications for over six years. He's also a member of the National Association of Newspaper Columnists.

Lu Pierro is a Creative Writing Major at Warren Community College. Her poems have appeared or are forthcoming in *Ars Poetica, Natural Awakenings, US1, Blast Furnace, If and Only If,* and *Threeandahalfpoint9, East Fork* among other journals. She is the recipient of both the Dodge Foundation Scholarship and the Dorothy E. Laurence Scholarship from the Fine Arts Work Center in Provincetown, Massachusetts.

Niles Reddick's collection *Road Kill Art and Other Oddities* was a finalist for an Eppie Award, his novel *Lead Me Home* was a national finalist for a ForeWord Award, a finalist in the Georgia Author of the Year Award in the fiction category, and a nominee for an IPPY Award. His work has appeared in anthologies *Southern Voices in Every Direction* and *Unusual Circumstances* and has been featured in many journals including *The Arkansas Review: a Journal of Delta Studies, Southern Reader, Like the Dew, The Dead Mule School of Southern Literature, The Pomanok Review, Corner Club Press, Slice of Life, Deep South Review, The Red Dirt Review, Faircloth Review, New Southerner,* and many others. His new novel, *Drifting too far from the Shore*, is forthcoming in 2016. His website is www.nilesreddick.com.

John G. Rodwan, Jr. is the author of *Holidays & Other Disasters* (Humanist Press, 2013) and *Fighters & Writers* (Mongrel Empire Press, 2010) and co-author of *Detroit Is: An Essay in Photographs* (KMW Studio, forthcoming in 2015). His poetry has appeared in journals including *Midwestern Gothic, Pacific Review,*

Pea River Journal, Red Earth Review, Riding Light Review, Thin Air and *Trickster.* 'The Shoes of the Old Man Are Some Clunky Slippers' first appeared in *San Pedro River Review,* Spring 2015.

Ruth Sabath Rosenthal is a New York poet, well published in literary journals and poetry anthologies throughout the U.S. and internationally. In 2006, Ruth's poem 'on yet another birthday' was nominated for a Pushcart prize. Ruth has authored 5 books of poetry: *Facing Home (a chapbook), Facing Home and Beyond, little, but by no means small, Food: Nature vs Nurture* and *Gone, but Not Easily Forgotten.* These books can be purchased from Amazon.com. For more about Ruth, 'Google' her and visit her website at www.newyorkcitypoet.com.

Mark Antony Rossi's poetry, criticism, fiction and photography have appeared in *The Antigonish Review, Another Chicago Review, Bareback Magazine, Black Heart Review, Collages & Bricolages, Death Throes, Ethical Spectacle, Gravel, Flash Fiction, Japanophile, On The Rusk, Purple Patch, Scrivener Creative Review, Sentiment Literary Journal, The Sacrificial ,Wild Quarterly* and *Yellow Chair Review.* More info at markantonyrossi.jigsy.com.

Carol Smallwood's most recent books include *Water, Earth, Air, Fire, and Picket Fences* (Lamar University Press, 2014); *Divining the Prime Meridian* (WordTech Communications, 2015); and *Writing After Retirement* (Rowman & Littlefield, 2014). Carol has founded, supports humane societies. 'Arrival' was first published in The Muse—An International Journal of Poetry December 2013, themuse.webs.com/dec%202013/Carol%20Smallwood.htm.

Carol Graf Snyder wrote 'What I'll Give You Since You Didn't Really Ask' in a master workshop led by Rachel Basch, author of *The Listener, Degrees of Love* and *The Passion of Reverend Nash.* She also worked on her novel, *A Sense of Place,* in Rachel's group. *The*

Litchfield Review published the prologue to the novel. Email her at snydercarol65@yahoo.com.

Lisa Solod (59) is the author/editor of *Desire: Women Write About Wanting* (Seal Press). Her essays and short fiction have been widely anthologized and published in numerous literary journals and magazines and she has been the recipient of several awards and fellowships. She has also been a successful working journalist whose credits include *Brain, Child* magazine, *The International Herald Tribune* and the *Boston Globe*. She is a regular contributor to *The Broad Side* and the *Huffington Post* and she can be found at middleagedfeminist.com. Solod is the author of the novel *Shivah*, currently a novel prize finalist, and is working on a collection of her essays. 'Yeah, But... I Still Feel Bad About My Face,' was originally published in *The Broad Side*. She lives in Savannah, Georgia.

Patty Somlo has received four Pushcart Prize nominations and has been nominated for Story South's Million Writers Award. Her essay, 'If We Took a Deep Breath,' was selected as a Notable Essay of 2013 for *Best American Essays 2014*. She is the author of *From Here to There and Other Stories*. Her second book, *Hairway to Heaven Stories*, is forthcoming in January 2017 from Cherry Castle Publishing. Her work has appeared in numerous journals, including the *Los Angeles Review*, the *Santa Clara Review*, *Under the Sun*, *Guernica*, *The Flagler Review*, and *WomenArts Quarterly*, among others, and in fifteen anthologies.

Keith Stewart's remarkable adventures usually occur near his hometown of Hyden in the hills of southeastern Kentucky, although he can be found aimlessly wandering the streets of nearby Lexington at any given moment. Before he shed his corporate casing, he worked as a certified public accountant for a multi-national company. He now enjoys less stressful work with much less pay, and blogs and writes and stuff. Oh, and he is as happy as a clam.

Margaret Stawowy's poetry has recently appeared in *Little Patuxent Review, Atlanta Review, Up the Staircase Quarterly*, and *Ginosko*. In the past year, she has won awards for her work from *Atlanta Review* and *Beyond Baroque*. Her current obsessions are genealogy and catering to the whims of her many potted plants. Contact her at pencilpusher89@hotmail.com.

Meneese Wall amalgamates various avocations inside her Santa Fe crucible—writer, graphic designer, wife, domestic slave, healthcare guru, and mother to a catalytic daughter (not necessarily in that order). "Seven Words" was first printed in *Buck Off Magazine*. More of her creative dexterity can be found on her website at www.meneesewall.com.

Clifford Wieck is the recipient of an Al Smith Individual Artist Fellowship and attended Bluegrass Writers Studio at Eastern Kentucky University.

Twice a Pushcart nominee, **Sarah Brown Weitzman** has been widely published in hundreds of journals and anthologies including *Poet & Critic, Art Times, The North American Review, Rattle, Mid-American Review, Ekphrasis, Abraxas, The Windless Orchard, Poet Lore, Potomac Review, Poem*, etc. Sarah received a Fellowship from the National Endowment for the Arts. A departure from poetry, her fourth book, *Herman And The Ice Witch*, is a children's novel published by Main Street Rag.

Anne Harding Woodworth (71) is the author of five books of poetry and three chapbooks, with a fourth coming out in early 2016. Her work is published widely in print journals and online. She lives in Washington, D.C., where she is a member of the Poetry Board of the Folger Shakespeare Library.

Changming Yuan, 8-time Pushcart nominee and author of 5 chapbooks (including *Kinship* 2015, and *Origin of Letters* 2015), is the most widely published poetry author who speaks Mandarin but writes English. Growing up in a remote village, Yuan began to learn English at 19 and authored several monographs on translation before moving to Canada. With a PhD in English, Yuan currently edits *Poetry Pacific* with Allen Qing Yuan at poetrypacific.blogspot. ca, and has poetry appearing in *Best Canadian Poetry*, *BestNewPoemsOnline, Cincinnati Review, Threepenny Review* and 1069 others across 36 countries.

About the Editor

Ashley Parker Owens (55) lives in the hills of Kentucky, where the gnomes are. She has lived in San Francisco in an ashram, and in Chicago where she helped with the Second Underground Press Conference and was the creator and editor of *Global Mail*. After the successful publication of Gnome Harvest by Double Dragon Publishing, Ashley is writing the next novels in the Gnome Stories Series, and completing a book of poetry called *Unveiling Creation*. She has an MFA in Creative Writing at Eastern Kentucky University and an MFA in Visual Arts from Rutgers University.

A special thanks to Susanne Braham for a final edit and proofread.

To submit works for a future anthology, go to http://kystory.net.

Made in the USA
Coppell, TX
25 May 2020